**Dedicated to advancing the education of every investor who has shared Wall Street-generated investment confusion and disappointment.**

# TABLE OF CONTENTS

PREFACE .................................................................................. vii
ACKNOWLEDGEMENTS ........................................................ xv
INTRODUCTION: Author Bob's Background ........................ xix
CHAPTER ONE: The relationships savvy investors avoid ............. 1
CHAPTER TWO: Old acquaintance remembered ...................... 21
CHAPTER THREE: An invitation to travel ................................ 39
CHAPTER FOUR: A trip to Africa at light speed ....................... 53
CHAPTER FIVE: A little market history and our present
    mutual fund debacle ............................................................. 71
CHAPTER SIX: Romance in bloom on the trip to Xiamggang? .... 89
CHAPTER SEVEN: Understanding ourselves as investors
    and reducing our frustrations ............................................. 105
CHAPTER EIGHT: Economic adventures in Vladivostok .......... 119
CHAPTER NINE: Personalities clash in the "Big Apple"! ......... 131
CHAPTER TEN: Bryce and Jane create their Utopia… ............. 147
APPENDIX ONE ..................................................................... 153
GLOSSARY ............................................................................. 165
FOR FURTHER READING ..................................................... 183
ABOUT THE AUTHOR .......................................................... 201
INDEX .................................................................................... 203
SUBJECT INDEX ................................................................... 205
SOURCE CREDITS ................................................................ 211

# Preface

There was no precise moment when I received the inspiration to write a book. Rather, many incidents led me to believe that there was a need for such a book. The leading brokerage firm I had joined boasted about their careful screening to match accommodations with very suitable surroundings and compatible companions for their three-month live-in educational program for trainees. I ended up with a middle-aged ex-New Yorker and a very young Floridian who had a passion for young women. Worse yet, we roomed on the tenth floor of the roach-infested Lexington Hotel that featured a single window air conditioner, inadequate water pressure, and elevators that functioned only half the time. The match was imperfect at best—the room a disaster. (I thought it some sort of corporate test of our loyalty!)

That first evening featured an *icebreaker* cocktail party held at headquarters for all the trainees. At that gathering, I noted the lack of professionalism that surrounded me.

It was not just the trainees, but also the instructors that left that impression. I recall saying to myself that I could "work around that obstacle." I would encounter many similar obstacles over the years. It was 1973, and the securities industry on Wall Street was morphing into something much less than it had been before "discount brokerages" emerged. The change was insidious, and the brokers would be the last to know. Thirty-five years later, many still do not yet understand how investors have been undermined. Yet, it is difficult to fault them since they follow their employer's dictates—like all good employees. It appears that after enough time passes, the process finds the salesperson surrendering to the disappointments and lack of understanding. The result is acceptance of the negative results as a matter of course. Increased regulatory control is needed.

Another memorable occasion occurred shortly after I returned from New York City after qualifying as a *registered representative* (stockbroker). The firm, of course, had assured all trainees that the firm's research was superior to any in the world. (Again, we cannot fault stockbrokers for their misinformation. Sadly, there is an abundance of vital information that those who hire them do not teach them. This is because a strong assumption exists on the part of the stockbroker that the employer has done the research and recommends only the best products and services. We were assured of that with great redundancy!) Again, more regulation is needed.

Since I was brought up in Toledo, Ohio, an important center for automotive manufacturing at the time, I naturally felt that I could learn a great deal by visiting with the firm's much-heralded automotive analyst. I telephoned the analyst and invited him to lunch. He accepted. At the designated time, I appeared at his *office*, a five-foot square cubicle with a Quotron stock quote machine and a single file cabinet. It was not the picture I expected, nor was it what the public had been led to believe. The fellow at the Quotron was a full twenty-seven years of age. Over lunch, I determined that he was a liberal arts graduate and had never worked at, or even visited, an automotive plant! (I was reminded of writer Paul Theroux's description of London's Grub Street as an enclave of not too respectable scribes.) It appears that analysts might also qualify as *pens-for-hire*. Again, I felt that this apparent weakness was yet another obstacle that I would have to work around. Another instance of poor regulation?

Upon my *graduation*, I returned from New York to the local office. The brokerage office had a telephone hookup with a small four by four inch speaker we termed the "squawk box." This device enabled the firm's most elite analysts to make stock purchase recommendations designed to incite sales. (The average leading brokerage house today requires that the broker gather minimum assets of $13 million the first year, during which period they are paid a *salary* with mandatory thresholds—*quintile rankings* which must be met.

The analysts normally targeted commission generating common stocks and *secondary offerings* of those Initial Public Offerings they had previously brought to market. There was always a proliferation of puffery concerning the economy, interest rates, currency exchange rates, etc. There was just enough solid information to convince one that these folks were *experts*. As part of our previous training, we were advised to structure a marketing plan to include influential parties that we considered centers of influence so that we could spread the brokerage firm's specialized knowledge among a wider foundation of investors and thus ensure our individual economic success. The results were consistently disappointing. The experience, however, had a single positive result—it taught me to do my own research whenever possible and ignore the highly vaunted opinions of analysts. I soon became an *in-house* analyst recommending stocks for my peers to buy, hold, or sell...and it worked well!

**...On the Importance of Honesty**

My dear wife Josephine has always shared my entrepreneurial interests. Before we were married, we had established an art import business that led us to a charming woman who owned a gift shop in our city and whose husband was the treasurer of a local corporation with several subsidiaries. He was a respected person in the financial world with whom we had only brief social interaction.

One afternoon I received a call from the treasurer requesting that I place an order for a quarter of a million dollars worth of Western Union preferred stock. That was a heady request for a rookie broker. However, if you are an economic aficionado, you may recall that, in 1973, interest rates were on the rise and the increase foreshadowed a two-year bear market. I had done some independent study and realized that rising interest rates were a negative for bonds because existing bond prices would have to adjust to match the higher interest rate paid on newer issues. Preferred stocks were, after all, bond surrogates and, as such, behaved similarly. I very tactfully advised my potential new client that it would not be wise to acquire the preferred stock at this time, and for those reasons. Unfortunately, he was quite indignant and stated that his broker at a competitor's brokerage house "would be happy to process the order!" I agreed that if he wanted to own the preferred stock, the other broker might be the best alternative. It was hard to say "no" to a quarter million dollar trade. Still is!

Eighteen months passed before I heard from the treasurer again. This time, he was a mellow fellow who asked if I made *house calls*, and I assured him that I could. He invited me to visit with the chief executive officer and him at their headquarters. While I was impressed with the rose-paneled office environment, I was more taken by the honest charm of the CEO. Over the course of a couple hours, I gathered a great deal of data on the family background of the owners of the corporation and their need for income. The CEO explained that their intention was to create a corporate bond portfolio valued at $2 million in an effort to provide interest income for the many family shareholders while affording portfolio stability. Once again, I had to say no. But, I was even more tactful this time, explaining that the IRS allowed *C corporations* a *dividends received exclusion* for corporations that invest in the stock, (not the bonds) of other C corporations. I pointed out that public utility preferred stock not only offered about equal interest income but also allowed for capital gains in the current declining interest rate environment.

I promised to research the opportunity further over the weekend, and we made an appointment for the following week. I reasoned that interest rate sensitive public utility stocks are usually quite stable. The research I wanted to complete was to determine whether the highest quality or modest quality preferred stocks performed the best during previous interest rate cycles. My conclusion over the weekend was that "A" rated preferred stocks experienced the greatest positive bounce. Dividends ran from 12%–14%, and the *dividend exclusion* and potential capital appreciation were simply frosting on the cake!

When we met the following Monday, the treasurer and the CEO agreed that my strategy was the best alternative and promised to follow my direction as I selected preferred stocks throughout the balance of the week. The next day, the treasurer telephoned my office and indicated that he had a problem. He advised me that they needed to invest $6 million, not $2 million! (I bit my lip as I silently thanked God.) Then, I explained that the stock market was big enough to absorb that amount of investment and that I would simply find several more utility preferred stocks to recommend.

## THE WALL STREET CASINO

The next few days, I positioned the $6 million account. I was advised that this was the largest such account at that local office in history. A little education, honest intent, and the ability to say "no" resulted in close friendships and a very productive relationship until the firm was sold years later. Such honesty and independent thinking remain the hallmark of <u>fee-only</u> advisors.

As I continued my independent study, I experienced many more such occasions that convinced me of the fact that common sense education based upon true experience, though contrary to the accepted brokerage advice, was sorely needed. Investors surely deserved better. I had the inclination to take action and further my successful research—an action that ran counter to my firm's desire.

I teamed up with my good friend Dick Laumann who was an information technology graduate at the local university. Dick and I explored the relationship among interest rates, inflation, and stock market cycles. We also enlisted the help of Dr. Henry Rennie who was Professor of Economics at the same university. Over the course of a few years, Dr. Rennie developed an econometric model that was uncanny in its ability to indicate market direction. This dual research led to my first book entitled *The Indicator!* which detailed the loose relationship between a combination of economic indexes (the Indicator) and stock market direction. Dick and I then developed the *Indicator! Newsletter* with the blessing of my broker/dealer. The newsletter made stock recommendations and employed *stop-loss* order points in order to safeguard subscribers against loss. Although the newsletter was a success, the maintenance, cost, and research requirements were onerous. This second book is intended to advance my studies, explode some Wall Street myths, and improve the investment performance of those who read it. There is not a household in America that is not threatened by the financial challenges of retirement.

I hope that your enjoyment of the story herein and the studied advice from *real life* will help you avoid errors such as the treasurer and millions of investors continue to make. We have provided present day "Author's Comments" and space for your notes at the conclusion of each chapter. In the event you have questions, please do not hesitate to write the publisher:

Technical Financial Publishing
P.O. Box 5194
Toledo, Ohio, 43611, USA

Yours for better investing,
Bob Kneisley, President, APR

# Acknowledgments

The Lord blessed my wife Jo and me with three children who, along with Jo, have always supported my sometimes exotic and rambling projects. Jo, of course, has been a major contributor and participant in this and other such projects. (The only one she ever denied was the gyrocopter!) Without her help on the home, business, and intellectual fronts, none of this would have been possible. Her love and devotion, and that of family members, have been an inspiration.

We owe a continued debt of thanks to those brokerage firms that I worked for far too long. They inadvertently allowed me the ability to search behind the doors for the true facts. This writing, will, unfortunately, reveal many less than savory facts about an industry that I had great respect for initially and for which I foster little respect for currently. The purpose, however, is to serve all investors with knowledge they deserve to know and benefit from. Authors who render independent advice that is far more useful than the "Wall Street experts" would surely include John C. Bogle, Gary Brinson, Eugene Fama, Kenneth French, Arthur Levitt, Burton G. Malkiel, Dave Ramsey, Gary Weiss, and David L. Wray. Many were studied in our research and some are featured in this book. We would suggest that you review their writings if you wish to maximize your opportunity to retire in style.

## ROBERT KNEISLEY

My entrepreneurial spirit was inherited from my late father. I admired him as I watched his business progress while raising five children after Mom died. I still admire him and his accomplishments today. He demonstrated the power of original thinking and often stated that successful people will frequently be found working while less successful people are relaxing. Benjamin Franklin's *Poor Richard's Almanac* mirrors the same belief in the statement, "Plow deep while the sluggard sleep, you shall have corn to sell and to keep." I have found it both enjoyable and productive to work evenings and weekends on things I love. This book is one such project.

On the academic side, I owe a debt of gratitude to adjunct University of Toledo professor Richard Laumann and to economist Dr. Henry Rennie for their early encouragement, research, and support—not to mention their warm friendships. My firm has certainly benefited from the sage advice from my friend Robert N. Rapp of Calfee, Halter & Griswold LLP and local attorney James S. Nowak. Research provided by Tom Roseen and Matthew Lemieux of Lipper Analytics, J. Bogle Research, and the financial academics at the University of Chicago Finance Department has been very helpful.

A young woman who helped to bring the original manuscript together was my colleague Ashley Wettle, who has reworked, massaged, and completed the somewhat complicated manuscript revisions that eventually resulted in this book. We thank brother Thomas R. Kneisley, daugh-

# THE WALL STREET CASINO

ter Kristene Hawk, writer Chris J. Bahnsen, author friends Ken and Bonnie Dickson, Northwestern Ohio Writer's Forum author Joan Repp, and my wife Jo for their editing effort. We are privileged to have traveled the path of life with all of these cherished family members and friends.

**ROBERT KNEISLEY**

# Introduction

**A Veteran Broker Illustrates the Myriad Pitfalls Investors Face Today...and Suggests Proven Alternatives**
by Bob Kneisley

Experience and study have convinced me that Modern Portfolio Theory provides an academically proven basis on which to build wealth. I am further convinced that the effort of the members of the "Wall Street Casino" to market past performance, stock picking, and market timing is a huge disservice to the public. Studies have demonstrated that the average growth mutual fund investor in the United States holds the fund for only 3 ½ years! While Wall Street sells last year's performance, enlightened fee-only advisors focus on controlling client expectations and educating clients so that they can remain invested long-term. The sole purpose of this book is to enlighten you so that you can do just that. It's your retirement. Plan to arrive in style!

The year was 1947, and my education was just beginning. It was a crisp, wintry morning. I awoke to my Dad chanting my name. I peeled back the covers and placed my naked feet bravely upon the cold floor. It was time to board my father's 1946 Ford and challenge the snowy weather to attend second-grade class. This morning, Dad's conversation alluded to *municipal bonds*. Dad explained the benefits: financing municipalities, providing tax-free income to investors, and the potential for investment growth. My father was a successful manufacturer of theater projection equipment and, like most children, I held his opinions in very high regard—still do! At first blush, it sounded like investing was a *sure thing*!

Consequently, I saved my money and, at age nineteen, I opened an account at a local brokerage firm and inquired of a stockbroker as to where I should place my $5,000 investment. The *knowledgeable professional* advised me to place that amount in a leading aircraft manufacturer's common stock. Within weeks, the manufacturer announced some 715 defects in its TFX Fighter Program and the stock cratered. I recall my frantic requests to place *stop/loss* or *limit* orders on the shares that I owned in an attempt to save principal. I received several disappointing return phone calls from the broker advising me that the stock had descended through those limit points and continued to fall. As you might guess, my first experience investing did not paint a pretty picture. Within weeks, I had lost 50% of my single stock portfolio value and simultaneously realized that I would have to gain 100% *just to break even!* An entire decade passed before I even thought of investing in another common stock. Instead, my attention focused on a more tangible investment in real estate.

# THE WALL STREET CASINO

Shortly after I was married, I began to search for a commercial real estate investment that could be leveraged with borrowed bank money. The leveraging was a necessity because I had so little cash. My wife and I found a mercantile building in South Toledo that had all the earmarks of a successful investment. I still felt that the respected opinion of my father was appropriate and compiled more than one brief for presentation and appeal. After two months of considerable persuasion, my father agreed that it might not be the worst investment I could ever make. My wife and I forged ahead and bought the building for $16,000. A scant four months later, the property across the street was purchased as the site for the Medical College of Ohio, a multimillion-dollar facility that would occupy more than thirty-five acres! As you might imagine, the inflation impact on our small building was very significant. We sold the property at a substantial gain a year or so later.

1946 Ford

Armed with that single experience, it occurred to me that *real estate securities* would be a reasonable compromise because the securities would provide day-to-day

TFX Fighter Plane

marketability, and the growth of real estate in the '60s was quite positive. An advertisement in the local paper led me to a securities underwriting firm in Cleveland that sold such real estate securities. I joined the investment banking firm as a "Series Six" licensed stockbroker and became division manager within two years. At that stage in my life, I was now married with two children and a mortgage on our home.

I must admit that, like you, I had witnessed the allure of glamorous *Wall Street* advertisements in magazines, newspapers, on radio, and on television, and I was impressed. Two years later, I saw an advertisement for stockbroker trainees for a major brokerage firm; I visited, submitted an application, and had a prompt interview, which went quite well. To my amazement, a week later, I was sequestered in a motel room with a psychologist who asked me searching questions about my family background. How was I to know that the effort was aimed at determining the investment potential of family and friends?

It did not take long for me to realize, however, that many of the products and strategies I was expected to present to clients were inferior investments. The only area that seemed to offer long-term benefits to clients was mutual funds. I became a very effective mutual fund salesman. While the clients did fine with their investments, my managers nonetheless insisted that I focus on the broad range of proprietary products. I resisted and eventually left that firm after nine years to start my own firm.

At about this time, the International Association for

## THE WALL STREET CASINO

Financial Planning was established, and I became a charter member of the Toledo chapter. About halfway through the certified financial planner course, I was confronted by another broker/dealer manager who wanted me to join yet another leading brokerage firm. I declined. After several months, he approached me again and indicated that his firm had a *financial planning* department in New York. That meant I could combine *state-of-the-art financial planning* with the mutual fund and brokerage business. Those advantages, combined with sluggish business at Kneisley Asset Management, caused me to give the proposal careful consideration. After several interviews, the manager offered a lump sum amount that was substantial enough to convince me that a change was appropriate. Unfortunately, thirty days after I joined the firm, they cancelled the entire financial planning department! Fate had just telescoped time back to my entry into the *Wall Street* brokerage melees.

My wife and I were by this time the proud parents of three children. I remained true to my convictions and continued to gather new assets to place in mutual funds. It was a hard business because mutual funds paid a commission only up front at that time—and they are long-term investments. They are not meant to be traded, and of course, I did not trade them. Instead, I became a master *harvester of money*.

Later, when we developed the *Indicator! Newsletter*, I bought my research on individual stock selections from a leading New York financial newspaper because they had a giant database that could identify those stocks that fit my selection criteria. The results for newsletter subscribers were good, but I could never get the research people to provide the selections at the bottom of their cycle. It finally became apparent that the newspaper publisher was also a Registered Investment Advisory firm. That is to say, when they provided recommendations based on my screening criteria, they *already* <u>owned</u> *these stocks!* Further, the newspaper also published several pages recommending the stocks that their readers should acquire. (Every stock chart I witnessed always showed a lower price to the left of the point at which their recommendation occurred.) Could it be that the investment advisor/publisher bought the stocks at $3 and recommended that the public buy them at $10? Sure could! This process is called "distribution" on Wall Street. And, it's legal!

We constructed several workable stock selection *models* only to find that they work miraculously well <u>for a period of time</u>, and then not well at all! I am convinced that the investing public is ill served by the *rotational* nature of institutional investment firms. My model criteria remained constant, but suddenly, the criteria were ineffective. Much like a *casino*, the game had changed. The process is called "rotation," and it still goes on today.

Surely, we all understand that if brokerage firm analysts could read the future, they would not need us to provide their revenue stream. We must further understand that institutional money managers that control billions of dollars daily do speak to each other within the tight enclave

# THE WALL STREET CASINO

we all know as "the Street." History has demonstrated and documented that people who wield control and power tend to monopolize trade. Institutional money managers are no different. They tell us that the markets are "rotational" (meaning that one sector can be driven up at the expense of another sector). That is why my models quit functioning.

In Las Vegas poker games, they call that "discarding" in an effort to improve your hand. After the managers jointly empower a particular sector, the *distribution channel* becomes you and I, the *investors*. To prove the efficacy of this statement, one could simply invest about $25,000 to subscribe to an institutional publication[1] that brings science to the study of institutional cash flows sector by sector and fund by fund. The newsletter is a very useful service for Wall Street's retail fund money managers!

---

1   It is a costly newsletter. (We were quoted $25,000 yearly.) The publication quantifies investment company cash flows thus aiding managers wishing to follow "cash flows" in an effort to outperform.

# ROBERT KNEISLEY

# Chapter One

"It's not buy for sell or sell for buy...but 'bye for now!'" exhorted Caesar Marmot, the greedy broker, as he whirled yet another sell order into the stockbrokerage office's pneumatic cylinder for prompt delivery to the office's wire room.

Intuitively, he recalculated his daily commission, which now totaled $1,250. With little emotion, he also noted the loss of approximately $20,000 to his client, the very beautiful Jane Cromwell. The broker held his commission total in higher regard than he did his clients! As he glanced around the brightly lit, ultra modern brokerage *pit*, he noted roughly thirty licensed salespeople busily espousing their various stories about securities they wished their telephone correspondents would aspire to own. Many, he knew, were

Jane Cromwell

1

## THE WALL STREET CASINO

much younger than he was because his office had a very high *sales executive* turnover rate. No wonder, since the firm required new hires to gather $10,000,000 in assets the first year! He chuckled at the truly *big hitters*. Most of them were standing with the telephone glued to their ear. He was well aware that most would stand all day. The rookies would laugh loudly in reverie, as they exclaimed, "Give me more rejection" after yet another series of unsuccessful cold calls. They often basked in the title "Cold Call Cowboy" if their manager felt that their outgoing telephone call rate was exceptionally high. It was a very tough business for the salesperson, and very often for the client as well.

The brokerage sales associates harbored an awkward camaraderie. While they were all competitors in their marketing area, they nonetheless established friendly relationships when they were not on the telephone. Their office featured a large lunchroom, which was a favorite gathering place to swap trade secrets and sales lore and joke about their prospecting experiences and often their clients.

Caesar Marmot would dazzle the *youngsters* with his success playing *Trivial Pursuit*. (What good can that do? "Trivial" is in the name!) More appropriate for the brokerage office was Caesar's oft quoted statement explaining the marvels of what Albert Einstein described as the eighth wonder of the world—compound interest.

He mused that if you double one penny every day for thirty days you will have $10,737,418.24! (While he was not as dumb as an ox, he was certainly no smarter.) He was,

# CHAPTER ONE

however, wonderful when it came to trivia. Younger sales representatives would listen intently over lunch while he explained such marvelous facts as "454 dollar bills weigh exactly one pound." Marmot knew exactly how many ridges existed on a U.S. dime (118) and even on a quarter (119). He loved to tell the story of the Dutch "tulip bulb mania" in Holland in the 1600s. He would explain redundantly the fact that in 1634, tulip bulbs were actually used as currency. (Such folly led to investors losing 99%!) He went on: "Frogs do not drink, and bullfrogs never sleep!" "A ten-gallon hat holds only a gallon." "Manhattan is the smallest county in America." His associates were spellbound. It was obvious to them—Caesar Marmot was an intellectual.

From time to time, traveling *wholesalers* (like snake oil salesmen) would visit the office to explain the *benefits* of some proprietary product or new *investment strategy*. If there was enough profit in the concept, they would rent a room at a local hotel and provide lunch for the brokers who attended. While entertaining, these meetings were not academically stimulating. On one occasion, they showed a film of a circus carousel with ponies consecutively labeled "stocks" and then "bonds." The intimation was simple—when stocks are up, bonds are down! When bonds are up, stocks are down! Unfortunately, most of the audience was able to grasp the wholly inaccurate concept. It was, of course, all about providing a basis for the sales staff to embrace any concept that might result in increased sales.

The year was 2000 and a bear market would soon ensue. Contrary to his firm's advertising claims, the broker had no vision as to what lay ahead. Perhaps remarkably, Ms. Cromwell was the broker's cousin on her father's side, nevertheless, was the object of his affection. He suspected, based upon solid facts, that she did not share his affection.

Our stockbroker, Mr. Caesar Marmot, was a pudgy forty-five-year-old product of a liberal arts education at an Ohio university. He weighed 238 pounds sans clothing (a repugnant thought). Quite non-athletic in appearance, he was affectionately known by the younger brokers in his office as "teaser the geezer" for reasons the reader must conjure. Mr. Marmot loved yachting and was a member of the area's prestigious yacht club. He captained a forty-five-foot Trojan yacht and was an active member of the local Power Squadron chapter. He was raised in a family of very modest means on the west side of Toledo. Although he elected to sign on with a leading broker/dealer, his broker dealer's educational process, like so many others, did not expose him to any review, let alone an intense study, of investment history. Matter of fact, the few classes he had in New York focused only on how to sell product.

Caesar Marmot

Mr. Marmot had been armed with just enough information to afford him the opportunity to convince a prospect

# CHAPTER ONE

of the legitimacy of his broker/dealer, the active management securities industry (retail brokerage), and the alleged high-end value of the products and services he offered. Like most stockbrokers, Caesar Marmot studied only the select material offered by his broker/dealer and the active management *retail* industry he served. He had been thoroughly immersed in the concept of *investment counseling* and the elite product and service standards espoused by the industry and his broker/dealer. Like all such professionals, he was rigidly controlled by his employer through the *compliance department*, the office manager, and several *self-regulatory*, but industry sponsored, agencies.

To suggest that he was a "salesperson" would be a personal affront. Any suggestion that he worked in a "boiler room" or "chop shop" operation would surely represent fighting words. In fact, Mr. Caesar Marmot had fallen into the retail brokerage trap—a very cleverly organized system of both mind and spirit control based upon the illusion of professional growth achieved through the instant gratification of monetary rewards (commissions). Such was the award for compliance to the established standards of his broker/dealer. The concept employs lavish rewards for outstanding production that include gifts, free trips (but taxable to the employee) to Cancun and elsewhere, "golden handcuff" retirement plans, and just enough secretarial support to keep the broker clawing toward the next level of production to match his/her increasing standard of living. It was an old and ruthless trick.

## THE WALL STREET CASINO

The retail brokerage industry has an acute understanding of human nature. They know that as one's income rises, one tends to elevate his/her standard of living. That is exactly the pattern that the industry encourages. The managers are also schooled to discourage in-depth research by the sales staff. (The firms claim instead that they pay large salaries to analysts for deep thought.) The manager, upon discovering a salesperson delving into academia that treads even remotely upon the alleged analyst's license, is reminded, "They are salespeople—not analysts"! Marketing efforts that follow the educational pattern, e.g., newsletter production by a broker, a television or radio interview, or a public appearance where media might be present are controlled through the compliance department and vague office *rules* that quell such freedoms. Retail brokerage is an autarkic industry that teaches its employees only that which benefits the office *bottom line*.

The psychological impact of instant gratification through the receipt of income directly related to the level of brokerage commissions is a very dynamic concept. The salespeople become conditioned much like Pavlov's dogs. The positive psychological impact becomes so repetitive and so powerful that the stockbroker will sometimes forego his/her important time spent with spouse and family. Our guess is that the lavish lifestyle encouraged by the industry also results in a high level of personal frustration and family turmoil.

And, with the on-going, fundamental need to increase his commission level, Marmot had a systemized approach to prospect induction. He even used the approach very effec-

# CHAPTER ONE

tively with Jane Cromwell. He would first explain his professional background in the most positive terms and inquire as to the needs and financial capability (free cash), as well as risk tolerance, of the prospect. He would then discuss the attributes of *active* portfolio management (leaning in a very self-serving fashion away from *passive* investments that pay no commission). This approach is, of course, necessary due to the industry's need to expand *active* management programs that generate needed *commission* income, excessive clearing costs, and other fees that are largely retained by the broker/dealer, not the salesperson. It is also why a 10% annual return on a retail growth mutual fund nets only a 6.7% return to the client after deduction of a 2.5% expense ratio and an inflation rate of 3.3%! Furthermore, mutual funds are not required to include their *clearing costs*, which can average an additional 2%–3% annually!

The April 2001 issue of *Financial Planning Magazine* details research by Mr. William J. Bernstein, publisher of the *Efficient Frontier Newsletter* concerning internal fees. Mr. Bernstein stated that the average actively managed large-cap mutual fund has annual fees and expenses of about 2%. For small-cap and foreign funds, the annual fees and expenses are about 4%, and the average micro-cap emerging-markets fund carries annual fees and expenses of almost 10%. *Passively* managed *index* funds are far less costly. Passive fund fees vary from 0.17% to 0.64%.

Caesar and Jane had many meetings wherein Jane, like most investors, was successfully indoctrinated into the *active management* camp. He had convinced Jane that pas-

## Percentage of Active Funds Outperformed by S&P Index Funds

Percent of Active Funds Outperformed by Asset Weighted Average Index Fund Return

| Fund Category | Comparison Index Fund Category | Last Quarter | One Year | Three Year | Five Year |
|---|---|---|---|---|---|
| Large Cap Blend Funds | S&P 500 Funds | 30.02 | 71.79 | 65.49 | 70.63 |
| Mid Cap Blend Funds | S&P MidCap 400 Funds | 86.11 | 45.33 | 60.78 | 62.12 |
| Small Cap Blend Funds | S&P SmallCap 600 Funds | 60.99 | 59.72 | 84.27 | 70.59 |

Percent of Active Funds Outperformed By Equal Weighted Average Index Fund Return

| Fund Category | Comparison Index Fund Category | | | | |
|---|---|---|---|---|---|
| Large Cap Blend Funds | S&P 500 Funds | 28.44 | 70.00 | 62.32 | 67.50 |
| Mid Cap Blend Funds | S&P MidCap 400 Funds | 84.72 | 29.33 | 50.98 | 59.09 |
| Small Cap Blend Funds | S&P SmallCap 600 Funds | 58.87 | 59.72 | 83.15 | 70.59 |

Source: Standard & Poor's. For periods ending March 31, 2007. ETFs are not included

## Lack of Performance Persistence

| Mutual Fund Category | Fund Count at Start Dec-03 | Percentage Remaining in Top Quartile Dec-04 | Dec-05 |
|---|---|---|---|
| **Top Quartile** | | | |
| All Domestic Funds | 512 | 41.60 | 15.23 |
| Large-Cap Funds | 271 | 37.27 | 15.50 |
| Mid-Cap Funds | 88 | 25.00 | 10.23 |
| Small-Cap Funds | 123 | 31.71 | 9.76 |

| | Fund Count at Start Dec-03 | Percentage Remaining in Top Half Dec-04 | Dec-05 |
|---|---|---|---|
| **Top Half** | | | |
| All Domestic Funds | 1023 | 61.78 | 37.83 |
| Large-Cap Funds | 541 | 58.60 | 32.16 |
| Mid-Cap Funds | 176 | 48.86 | 27.27 |
| Small-Cap Funds | 245 | 46.53 | 25.71 |

Source: Standard & Poors. For Periods Ending December 31, 2005

sive management was simply a <u>random</u> selection of securities that are held for a period matching the investment time horizon required by the client. He explained, on the other hand, that active portfolio management entailed the construction of a portfolio using both traditional and *modern*

# CHAPTER ONE

| Mutual Fund Category | Fund Count at Start Dec-01 | Percentage Remaining in Top Quartile ||||
|---|---|---|---|---|---|
| | | Dec-02 | Dec-03 | Dec-04 | Dec-05 |
| **Top Quartile** | | | | | |
| All Domestic Funds | 482 | 60.58 | 21.58 | 16.39 | 5.81 |
| | | | | | |
| Large-Cap Funds | 266 | 47.74 | 9.02 | 6.39 | 1.88 |
| Mid-Cap Funds | 71 | 53.52 | 5.63 | 4.23 | 0.00 |
| Small-Cap Funds | 129 | 46.51 | 13.95 | 10.08 | 3.10 |

| | Fund Count at Start Dec-01 | Percentage Remaining in Top Half ||||
|---|---|---|---|---|---|
| | | Dec-02 | Dec-03 | Dec-04 | Dec-05 |
| **Top Half** | | | | | |
| All Domestic Funds | 964 | 71.37 | 36.10 | 29.46 | 17.63 |
| | | | | | |
| Large-Cap Funds | 531 | 64.78 | 25.42 | 19.77 | 11.68 |
| Mid-Cap Funds | 142 | 63.38 | 21.13 | 16.90 | 10.56 |
| Small-Cap Funds | 258 | 72.09 | 31.01 | 21.32 | 12.02 |

Source: Standard & Poor's. For Periods Ending December 31, 2005

strategies to include the direct management and control of the portfolio to meet the client's objectives. (He cleverly avoided detailing any internal and external cost factors that impact active management performance very heavily as alluded to on page 7 and above.) We shall discuss those negative aspects in more detail later.

He also carefully avoided any discussion concerning solutions to *problem investments*, commissions, expense ratios, investment policy statements, investment quality standards, portfolio return measurement, and portfolio performance considerations. He focused his educational process on *diversification* rather than proper *asset allocation*, and, even then, with unrecognized *overlap* of securities within the several funds he recommended. Oh, and he explained that the dot over the "i" is a "tittle," a "twit" is actually the techni-

## THE WALL STREET CASINO

cal term for a pregnant goldfish, and a "jiffy" is 1/100 of a second—all that, just to prove his vast knowledge.

Properly conceived, asset allocation is the deliberate division of a portfolio into various asset classes. These might include U.S. bonds, foreign securities, U.S. stocks, short-term securities, and even securities that represent tangibles such as gold or real estate. The goal of asset allocation is <u>preservation of capital and controlled volatility</u>. His discussions, however, were about *diversification* that focuses on investment in various vehicles *within* such asset classes. Worse yet, as a salesman, he was forced to select vehicles that <u>recently</u> performed well (and may quite possibly be on the crest of a downturn). Such vehicles most frequently include individual stocks or actively managed, *commission-way* mutual funds rather than the more efficient *index products* that are passively managed investments. Since mutual funds are the preferred vehicle, the first table above illustrates the percentage of *actively managed* funds that were *outperformed* by S&P index funds. Note that after five years, a full 59%–70% of funds are losers relative to index funds. Could this help explain why investors do not hold funds longer term?

Standard & Poor's did the above studies. They keep quarterly data on *active* versus *passive* funds. Their reports show the many advantages of passive management and are unique in that they correct for *survivorship bias*[2] when com-

---

2   survivorship bias: the liquidation or merger of a poor performing mutual fund allowing improved performance rankings of the remaining funds in the family

# CHAPTER ONE

paring mutual fund performance. Average returns for fund groups are often calculated by other databanks with *equal weighting*, which results in the returns of a $10 *billion* fund affecting the average with the same weight as a $10 *million* fund. Standard & Poor's asset-weighted methodology is a far more accurate assessment of how investors fared. They also employ returns-based style analysis to classify funds across different time horizons.

The middle table above illustrates various fund categories based upon performance persistence over a three-year period. The table suggests that the great majority of leading funds are no longer top performers after only three years! There is no predictability. Yet, *Money* magazine continues to publish the "top performing mutual funds" every year, costing investors' performance and distorting their financial attitudes. It is what financial author Jane Quinn describes as "financial pornography"! The final table above demonstrates that over a five-year period, the funds that remain in the top quartile are even far fewer.

## A Host of Investor Problems

Other areas that present problems with the structure and marketing of retail mutual funds include the many share "classes" now available. So many often confuse investors and can be very misleading.

In addition, mutual funds, unlike passively managed accounts do not feature tax deductible fees and commissions. Using a fee-only investment advisor permits the deduction of custodian, management and advisor fees while allowing extreme "quantity discounts" on fees for larger investors. And, the operating costs of retail funds are slow to come down.

"Marketing fees" paid to the brokerage offices that distribute retail mutual funds add an additional profit center for the broker/dealer that, very often, is not understood, or recognized, by the sales person who sold the fund.

While the "hidden fees" of retail funds appear to be declining slightly, they are still a major drag on performance over time, (and again, these fees are NOT tax deductible.)

IPO leveraging: When a fund family acquires newly issued "initial public offering" shares they need not say which fund the shares will ultimately be owned by. They can hold the shares to determine a positive outcome and then allocate them to a small float fund to enhance return.

Confusing fund names can cause investors to conclude that the fund's style is actually at odds with the funds investment objective. Style drift is a similar problem. Drift occurs when the manager seeks to improve returns by straying from the style to attempt to enhance fund performance.

Manager changes do not require investor approval. A new manager can have a significant impact on the performance of a retail fund. Some managers manage on a "part-time" basis, some have invested within their personal brokerage accounts while buying the same shares for the retail mutual fund.

Then there is the conflict presented by what the trade refers to as "soft dollar" payments by retail mutual fund

# CHAPTER ONE

sponsors to brokerages for sales advantage and "bonuses" paid by broker/dealers to their sales staff to place "proprietary" funds with investors. And the list of shortcomings goes on.

Regardless of the above facts, Mr. Marmot spent an inordinate amount of time explaining the fundamentals of security analysis and the accuracy of his firm's professional analysts. He had explained that security analysis involves the gathering and organizing of logical information into a framework and then using that framework to determine the *intrinsic value*[3] of a security. He stated that the intrinsic value provides a means of accurately measuring the value of a security! Be aware that accounting data are always obsolete, if not somewhat inaccurate in many aspects. *Technical* and *fundamental* analyses are based upon linear projections and the belief that somehow the analysts can portend the future. Again, if they could accomplish that, they would not need investors, would they?

Mr. Marmot obviously believed that markets are inefficient and that mispricing can be easily determined through fundamental analysis. This belief is largely unsupported by the twenty-two Nobel laureates in the area of finance at the University of Chicago. Indeed, Eugene Fama, of the university, holds that any security analysis is capable of identifying mispriced securities with a frequency that would about equal random chance alone! The glaring ad-

---

3   The actual value of a company or an asset based on an underlying perception of its true value including all aspects of the business, in terms of both tangible and intangible factors.

vantage of passive investing lies in the fact that it does <u>not</u> depend upon the need for analysts at all.

Jane would later understand that, as a salesperson, Mr. Marmot was not regulated by the Investment Advisor's Act of 1940. The act applies to licensed investment advisors and requires that the prospect receive a full written disclosure (Forms ADV Part II) of information about the advisor's background, education, operational details, services offered, and conflicts of interest. Licensed advisors are held to a much higher fiduciary standard regarding their clients' interests than are *stockbrokers* (or whatever title their firm might deem appropriate). Importantly, since the fee charged by the advisor is dependent upon the success of the investment, the investment advisor is *on the same side of the desk* as the client. We know of no *fee-only* investment advisors that offer proprietary product. Nor do they charge commissions, accept *marketing fees* from the investment managers they recommend or offer retail products and services. These are some of the detrimental attributes that broker/dealers offer.

At each meeting with Jane, Mr. Marmot exhibited an ulterior motive that was emotionally driven. When he visited with Jane, he always suggested the possibility of a more personal relationship. He had invited her on many dates. While she was always appropriately delicate in her refusal, she did find his insistence undesirable and ultimately called off several future meetings because of his demands.

Caesar Marmot, however, had impressed Jane with his

# CHAPTER ONE

correct explanation that stocks represented ownership in a corporation while bonds represented an I.O.U. certificate issued by a corporation to the bond investor. He also accurately explained that stock warrants are similar to long-life *options* with maturities as far out as twenty years. He stated that they frequently are issued as "sweeteners" with bond issues. Caesar explained that the bond warrant gives the bondholder the right to purchase a certain number of shares of the corporation's stock at a stipulated price for a specific period of time. He said the warrants generally traded at a relatively low unit cost and that their biggest attraction was the leverage they offer if the underlying stock moves up in value. Mr. Marmot made it clear that warrants, like stock option *puts* and *calls*, are a form of derivative security. Jane understood that they derive their value from the price behavior of some other real or financial asset.

Then the broker explained in detail the application of call options[4] as a means of *renting* the individual stocks that exist in Jane's Cromwell Family Trust. The rental concept was an absolute stroke of genius that was purely understandable to any prospect. It, however, did not illuminate a glaring difference between real estate and options. Options have a very short-term expiration, whereas rental real estate is a long-term investment opportunity. As always, it is not how much you earn so much as it is how much you

---

4   A strategy whereby the investor sells the option contract giving the buyer the right to acquire the security at an agreed price within a time limit.

## THE WALL STREET CASINO

keep. Mark Twain famously said, "I am not so concerned as to the return *on* my money as I am concerned about the return *of* my money."

# CHAPTER ONE

# Notes

## THE WALL STREET CASINO

# Author's Comment

So there you have it...the truth about a multi-billion dollar institution known as the retail broker/dealer industry lacking proper regulation. Worse yet, they and the investment bankers contribute billions to our political candidates!

Artemus Ward, a nineteenth century writer, wryly stated, "It ain't the things we don't know that get us in trouble, it's the things we know that ain't so." If the reader would allow me to paraphrase, I would say that it is virtually impossible to <u>teach</u> someone who feels they already know it all. The billions spent by Wall Street institutions (to include the retail mutual fund industry) on advertising in every possible medium seem to have coerced our consciousness into the acceptance of the paradoxical fact that, even though we have accumulated great wealth, we are somehow comfortable taking investment advice from those whose educational background we have not vetted.

As I write, it is July 2008, and a major concern for our economy centers around the possibility that the drop in home valuations will find thousands of homeowners simply walking away from their undervalued property, which will then be foreclosed and result in a fire sale by the mortgage lender. Unfortunately, it is a scenario that can spiral into a deeper recession. Remember that we went through the same unregulated savings and loan catharsis roughly sixteen years ago? Where are our regulators?

Could there be a nexus between the old Wall Street axiom that investors are driven by either fear or greed? Does it then follow that if you reduce fear, that you increase greed? The current real estate speculation and subsequent "sub-prime mess" in 2008 provide a gripping illustration.

# CHAPTER ONE

## 1977 and the Seed of Destruction?

*Louis S. Ranieri started his career in Salomon Brothers' mailroom and became the "father of securitization" when he created the first private pool consisting entirely of home loans in 1977. I am sure that he never could have guessed that the pool would become the core of Wall Street's marketing efforts that distributed sub-prime mortgages to the investing public. The outcome is yet another example of the Street's employees feeling that they could act as mere agents to build their wealth, ignoring any sense of liability.*

**ROBERT KNEISLEY**

# Chapter Two

Caesar made every effort at every possible turn to charm Jane Cromwell into ever-increasing investments with his firm. Not unlike other salespeople in the retail brokerage business, Caesar *usually* recommended investments based on their past *track record*. People like to invest in securities that have done well. Thus, they are often *sold* securities trading at their peak! The Cromwell trust portfolio was comprised of individual stocks, bonds, cash, retail mutual funds, with a smaller percentage placed in call options and a *wrap* account with the firm's proprietary money manager. Over the years, as the market rose, so too did the Cromwell Family Trust portfolio. The portfolio rose at a slower pace, however, due to the drag of commissions; retail mutual fund clearing costs; the identified, internal *expense ratio* of the retail mutual funds; custodian fees; and the fees levied by the wrap account manager.

It is important to note that only some of the above fees generated within the portfolio by the retail brokerage industry were tax-deductible. (The total management fees as well as custodial fees and advisor fees for the separately managed wrap account are fully tax deductible.) The lack of fee deductibility, of course, was not highlighted in any discussion between Jane and Mr. Marmot. This seems an all too typical retail brokerage exclusion.

Even though Caesar was a relative, he had been a "friend of the family" so to speak for many years, and that fact seemed to belie his insensitivity toward the losses he recently dealt to the Cromwell family, and in fact, to Jane, the woman he felt he loved. Caesar glanced down at his wristwatch. He noticed it was Wednesday and once again, he placed his traditional telephone call to the lovely Jane Cromwell to invite her to join him for dinner that weekend.

Caesar had a somewhat remarkable mole located about one inch down and an inch back from his right ear. The mole was topped with a rapidly growing black hair that, as you might imagine, created no end of tedious effort when he tried to shave. The good news is that when he was contemplating an important decision, he often would twirl the hair between his thumb and index finger. This seemed to help him reach a conclusion in a shorter period of time. He was doing that now as he contemplated his approach with Jane on the telephone. Apparently feeling a need for self-castigation, he dialed the phone with nervous excitement.

Across town, Jane Cromwell was reclining in her study, enjoying her freshly baked pandowdy (for real). It was a

# CHAPTER TWO

chilly evening in March and the fireplace provided some comforting warmth as she reviewed her brokerage statement. (She, like most of us, abhorred brokerage statements of any kind. This was so because they have never been understandable and no amount of counseling could help her understand the true performance of the trust account.) Jane was convinced that the statements were *designed to defy understanding* so that the sales representative had more control. The more she thought about broker Marmot's lack of concern regarding the family trust's recent losses, the more infuriated she became. "How can family treat family so?" she questioned.

Jane's thoughts reverted to her happy college days with Bryce. The year was 1981 as she recalled his arrival in what was, even then, an ancient Plymouth convertible to whisk her off to his fraternity party. She recalled the controlled craziness and interesting personalities that always surrounded her at those events. Bryce seemed a center of influence, which made Jane a local attraction as well. Bryce enjoyed visiting with Jane's mom and they had many conversations on a wide range of topics. He kept in touch with Jane and her mom by e-mail on a regular basis over the years. Jane realized now that she still had a very deep affection for her college friend. Sadly, in their senior year, class schedules

Bryce Cunningham

conflicted with their relationship. Shortly after graduation, Bryce found employment that took him to New York and the two drifted apart.

Every calendar quarter, Jane and her parents received a newsletter from her old college friend's investment advisory firm. The event always aroused positive emotional response when she reflected upon her past relationship with Bryce. These were indeed fond memories. But, the contents of the newsletter seemed a distant foreign language! Given Marmot's education effort, such terms as "passive investment" (holding of broadly diversified securities in an effort to provide "Free Market" investment returns), and "capital asset pricing model" (a model that describes the relationship between risk and expected return on a security) seemed senseless to Jane. Adding "alpha" (measure of performance on a risk-adjusted basis), "beta" (a measure of a stock's volatility), and the failure of "active portfolio management" (retail mutual fund management) was simply inexplicable verbiage to Jane. Thus, she normally reviewed the letters but often disregarded them. Her thoughts of Bryce, though, and his always positive attitude, warm smile, and caring ways would sometimes linger in her mind for several pleasurable hours.

Now the late afternoon sun cast long, oblique shadows across the lawn as Jane reminisced about her college love. He was so intelligent, honest, and caring. These were emotions she longed for now. She mentally contrasted what were then his thoughtful ways with those of her brokerage connection, Caesar Marmot. Bryce Cunningham, unlike

## CHAPTER TWO

Caesar, seemed sensitive to the needs of anyone he met. She remembered that he was in the School of Finance at college. He was a very attractive 170 pounds with brown hair, blue eyes, and an athletic build.

Jane recalled that Caesar was a two-hundred-pound liberal arts major in college and ended up being a weight-gaining stockbroker. She chuckled as she recalled that Caesar did not graduate in the top half of his class. Rather, he was one that made the top half possible! Since Bryce did graduate with honors and was an avid boating enthusiast, Jane wondered if he was still a boater. He would surely be a true success in the area of finance. She sighed, smiling in the full knowledge that Bryce would be very successful at anything he put his mind to.

As she looked down at her brokerage statement, she noted the substantial losses. The trust portfolio now seemed a field of thorns! Her frustration became manifest. Jane crumpled the statement tightly and hurled it into the fireplace. Watching with cynical satisfaction as the statement shriveled in the flames, she drifted off into a deep sleep. The phone rang...

To Caesar Marmot's great dissatisfaction, the insistent phone went unanswered. Now, with the tender strains of Toots Thielemans' "La Vie En Rose" seemingly in the background, the diminishing light rays underscored Jane's loveliness as they highlighted her stylish brunette hair with a golden sheen. Jane was thirty-seven years old with a fair complexion and an attractive figure. She was an avid

## THE WALL STREET CASINO

jogger weighing 117 pounds and was 5' 2". She was a business graduate of the local university and a shareholder in the very successful Cromwell Greenhouse Enterprise. A wholesaler, the firm was a corporate entity with subsidiaries in five states. The family entrusted Jane and her mother with the responsibility of investing the $5 million in assets of the family trust. The recent poor performance of the stock market was constantly featured in every news media imaginable. Concern for the family's assets was the primary cause of Jane's stress now. Frustration being the mother of despair, solace was finally offered by her deeper sleep.

As the blue-yellow fireplace flames painted silhouettes on the ceiling, Jane noted a very strange curiosity. Rising in the shadows beyond the flickering flames appeared a contorted image of what seemed to be Bryce Cunningham accompanied by a much older man.

The evening news portended even greater disaster. The stock market report (far too similar to the daily sports tally) announced that the Dow Jones Industrial Average declined by a full six hundred points! Jane was numb! Frantic, she rushed to her computer and attempted three times to type her access code to reveal the value of the family trust portfolio. Success revealed failure. Trust portfolio losses now exceeded 30%. The $5,000,000 portfolio was now valued at only $3,400,000—a loss of $1,600,000! Even the aforementioned *call options* Caesar had written against many stock positions offered little protection against such an onslaught. (You will recall that he had cleverly used real estate income

## CHAPTER TWO

to illustrate how the family trust stocks could be *rented out* for cash to *speculators* who could then acquire the underlying stock if it rose dramatically. Caesar was willing to take this risk with the trust assets that were profitable.) "Stock rental income indeed!" mumbled Jane.

The following morning, Jane frantically called the brokerage office number. It seemed an eternity before the soothing voice of the receptionist answered. Jane asked for Mr. Marmot. Her voice trembled with fear. "One moment, please," the receptionist oozed.

"Caesar here," answered the broker with the clarity of a shard of crystal but in a cheerful tone.

"What is happening to the market?" asked Jane.

"Jane! Great to hear from you! The market is reacting to a major sell-off for no apparent reason. Our analysts feel that the downturn is only temporary. Jane, we see this as a buying opportunity. Do you have any sideline cash we can apply?"

"Caesar, you will be ice skating in hell before I commit additional funds to this roulette game! Besides, we don't have any extra cash right now," she sighed.

Caesar nervously manipulated the mole hair on his neck as he contemplated how he might ask Jane for time together under such negative circumstances.

"Another opportunity lost, Jane. Do you want to sell now or hold?" Caesar queried.

Jane hesitated for a moment, reflecting on her father's wise statement when he had suggested that they would only have *paper losses* if they held their portfolio positions. Real loss occurs when they liquidate. Jane was beginning to feel that the whole system was simply a giant poker game as she answered Caesar. "I'll hold," she stated with a grimace (as she realized the term actually was poker jargon).

"Very well, Jane. Lunch tomorrow?" inquired the broker as he unconsciously pulled on his tight shirt collar. Jane summoned her composure once again and graciously declined.

A better idea had occurred to her. She knew she had Bryce's New York phone number. She would retrieve his newsletter from her file and try to locate her old flame and financial guru to renew their friendship and maybe gain a second opinion regarding the plight of her family's nest egg. She now hungered for more independent advice, and her college friend Bryce was always able to sort through exactly the quagmire of information, hype, and pure *noise* she now seemed to encounter at every turn.

As Jane thought about calling Bryce, her excitement heightened. It was like her first eighth-grade date! As then, she sat for several moments contemplating what she would say to Bryce after all these years and what her retort might be to his responses. She hummed the tune "Sentimental Journey," and her heartbeat accelerated as she carefully pressed the numbers on the phone.

"Hi! This is Bryce!"

"Hello, Bryce. This is Jane Cromwell calling after all these years. How are you?"

## CHAPTER TWO

"You have got to be kidding! Jane, it is great to hear from you! I'm just fine, thank you."

"Great to hear your voice as well, Bryce," Jane responded. "Bryce, are you now a boater as well as a financial advisor?"

"Jane, I am flattered by your question. You have a great memory. I'm not sure how success is measured, Jane, but my partner and I have enjoyed our investment management business for some twelve years now, and our *passive* investment strategies seem to be working very well for our clients. Oh, and we have a bigger boat too!"

"Bryce, that's great news! And, that's pretty much why I am calling you. I really need your financial advice concerning our family trust and wonder if you might be coming west any time soon?"

"Your timing is propitious! As a matter of fact, we plan to come to your fair city on Monday. We'll be there for several weeks to visit with clients. Would you care to visit at that time?"

"That would be wonderful!" Jane exclaimed as her heart leapt several beats. Jane provided her current address and phone numbers—even her fax number. She was so eager to see Bryce again and to meet his associate that the next week seemed months in passing.

Sadly, the week truncated a year's worth of negative market action into just a few days. But, on Monday morning, the rising sun suggested a more positive environment. On this day, Jane expected to hear from Bryce. She felt secure in the thought that visiting with Bryce and his business partner would be a positive experience and could possibly ease her stress level concerning the stock market and the family trust. So convinced was Jane that she drove to work with a newfound appreciation of her surroundings and a smile on her face. As her mind wandered, so too did the direction her vehicle tracked as she momentarily traveled left of center.

It was 10:30 when Jane's cell phone heralded the arrival of Bryce and Mr. Smith. Bryce was cheerful and dominated the conversation, explaining that they had met with their client and suggesting that they meet for lunch the next day. Jane promptly agreed. The next day, Bryce and his partner Adam Smith arrived early and made arrangements with the hostess regarding seating and the check. They waited in the reception area for Jane's arrival. Bryce remembered Jane with fondness, but not with the tenderness that Jane experienced.

Jane arrived on schedule and was very pleased to renew her acquaintance with Bryce and meet his business partner. She was impressed with Bryce's appearance and demeanor but was somewhat taken aback by Mr. Smith's appearance. He had long gray hair and wore a dark cloak, a circa 1800 white shirt, and black trousers—not unattractive in appearance but surely gaunt.

When they were seated, they proceeded to recount their col-

*Adam Smith*

## CHAPTER TWO

lege experiences, and Bryce explained his firm's independent approach to investing. While Jane was impressed with his presentation, she found it hard to accept his opposition to just about everything concerning investments that she had learned from her broker. Rather, she had a stubborn conviction regarding the positive nature of leading broker/dealers, insurance firms, and the billions they spend on advertising to support their cause. She shared the views, of course, of the majority of American citizens. Mr. Smith counseled, stating that, "therein lies the flaw."

His position irritated Jane to the point of challenging Mr. Smith's expertise relative to the broad base of knowledge possessed by the broker/dealer community. Mr. Smith and Bryce took her lament in stride. They had been there before. While in disagreement, Jane was impressed with the way Bryce constructed his words and thoughts into a fabric of logic that was hard to dismiss. She, however, was not convinced of his position regarding *independent* financial advisory advice versus the Wall Street establishment with which she was dealing.

Both Bryce and Mr. Smith long ago accepted the position that the broker/dealer community had committed an historic error when the progress of the NASDAQ[5] electronic stock exchange resulted in *negotiated commissions* on May 1, 1975. Adam Smith explained that growth mutual funds were no longer *long-term* investments because the managers of the funds were *churning* the mutual funds

---

5   National Association of Securities Dealers' Automated Quotation System

internally, creating enormous profit for retail brokerages in the form of clearing costs (commissions). Jane was noticeably irritated. On occasion, Adam Smith would refer to some obscure "oceans of opportunity" as though that would provide Jane with the solution she needed. And Bryce always wholeheartedly agreed.

After lunch, Jane noted that the volatile stock market continued its decline and further pain was inflicted upon the family trust. Jane's stress was compounded upon learning from her father that her dear mother had been diagnosed with leukemia. She was devastated and became despondent for several days. Meanwhile, Bryce and Adam continued to try to enlighten her regarding wealth building. Not accepting their sage concepts had no impact whatsoever on her growing affection for Bryce. He, however, was targeting her investment intellect, trying to convince her that there is a more efficient way to conserve and build wealth. He and Adam continued to emphasize concepts that had been proven academically as well as in real life—and with real cash. They often referred to Professor Harry Markowitz, a student from the University of Chicago who later won a Nobel Prize for his concepts that led to what is now known as Modern Portfolio Theory†.

It was late that evening when Jane returned home. She was exhausted and felt as though she was falling into a state

---

† a theory that optimizes expected return based on a given level of risk

## CHAPTER TWO

of mild depression due to her mother's illness coupled with the negative stock market performance she was experiencing. She sought sleep as a refuge. As she slipped into the solitude that sleep normally brings, she felt herself falling rapidly into a dark and shadowy chasm unlike anything she had witnessed before. As she slipped down the slope, she could make out an emerald pool with a slick, shiny shoreline. Wisps of blue green fire seemed to be emanating, almost like rising steam from the surface of the pool. The pool itself, though quite beautiful, was bubbling as though it might be boiling. She desperately clutched at the inclined surface as she descended, with painful slowness, inexorably toward the pool. She was terrified as her body sank into the unknown liquid.

The pond had an acrid odor and her skin tingled as though it were immersed in turpentine. She feared that the pond might be acidic and that she would soon die. She dog paddled back to the shoreline in an effort to keep the liquid off her face. But every shore she approached was hot with the fiery green flames. After several frantic minutes, she came to a portion of the shoreline that featured a jagged rock formation and was able to gain a foothold and climb frantically from the pond, only to note as she glanced about that the pond had suddenly grown to three times its original size. She had to step away from the wispy flames lest she burn her flesh as she tried to leave the area. Within twenty feet of the pond, the flames subsided, and she found herself in an area of green undergrowth overlooking a small town with scarcely any electric lighting at all. What light she did note seemed to have the apparition of "the spirit of success" she saw earlier in the glow of her fireplace. On closer inspection, the apparition looked a great deal like Bryce's partner, Adam Smith!

The terrifying saga ended as Jane awakened and realized she had experienced a nightmare. She breathed a sigh of relief as she became aware that the dream must relate to her trying circumstance. She was certain that the emerald pool represented the vicious stock market she was experiencing, and she, in fact, was the physical symbol of her mother or family trust portfolio sinking into the mire. (A bear market creates such nightmares for millions of retail *active management*[6] investors.)

Much like the ebb and flow of life's rollercoaster of euphoria and grief, investors experience similar sensations. As we ascend on the rails of the rollercoaster, we hear the comforting click–click of the descent locks. All is well when market volatility is upward. But as you know, once at the apex, the screaming begins as the volatility, (standard deviation), reverses, and we all feel we are facing certain doom. This analogy is not lost on typical investors when they too arrive at the valley where many exit their investments at the *bottom* of the market. And, they may never return again!

The villain, of course, is not the rollercoaster itself but rather the up and down volatility that drives investors

---

6   a mutual fund manager's attempt to enhance investment performance by investing in what appears to be undervalued securities.

## CHAPTER TWO

to miss the grand opportunity to build wealth. The retail brokerage industry entices investors to "buy high and sell low." Emotions rule the day and abundant commissions are generated for those controlling "the Street." Again, this is a concept many present salespeople cannot grasp.

An analogy Bryce used to illuminate the impact of volatility envisioned one's own residence. "If a fellow were to place a sign in your front yard each day that listed the value of your home, you would be distracted by the fact that the home's value changes in price on even an hourly, let alone daily, basis. If the fellow continued to place the daily sign, you would probably sell the property within months!" It is no different with any commodity including securities. We must view investment with a long-term perspective—and with a minimum of emotion.

## ROBERT KNEISLEY

# Notes

## CHAPTER TWO

# Author's Comment

*It is true. Bear markets can result in extreme* lower back pain *for all investors. Passive investors normally suffer much less. It would appear that our lovely protagonist has fallen into an attitude of pernicious stress. This problem is the normal result of the psychological fears of investors compounded by the fact that the* institutional *investor dominates markets. Worse yet, their* rotational *investment style causes very wide price swings as they move from one investment sector to another. The net result can be extremely painful to investors who opt to invest in individual stocks. In my thirty-five plus years in the industry, I have created over four* investment models *or* trading systems. *They worked well for a limited period, after which their functionality collapsed. I finally realized that the* system *did not fail. Rather, it must be the* rotation *of retail mutual fund managers who had simply moved to another investment sector, like changing the game in Las Vegas. This is just another reason why* active management *in any form can be damaging to your investment health.*

*Are hedge funds better?*

*The 2006 annual report for Berkshire Hathaway featured Mr. Warren Buffet (declared the richest man in the world in 2008) expressing his disdain for what he termed "grotesque" internal fees that investors were forced to pay when owning mutual funds and hedge funds. A close aide to Mr. Buffet stated that Mr. Buffet wagered $320,000 in January 2008 on the premise that an S&P 500 index fund would outperform any group of hedge funds over the next decade. He got a taker for the gamble, and each put up $320,000, which was invested in a zero-coupon bond that would mature at $1 million in ten years. Time will*

## THE WALL STREET CASINO

*tell. We understand that Mr. John Bogle, founder of Vanguard Funds Group, made a similar wager over a five-year period ending in 2000. Mr. Bogle pocketed $25 on the friendly bet. In light of our current economic/political travails, I have to ask "ízzat faire?" Please allow me to explain.*

*Laissez faire, as you know, is a French phrase describing an economic doctrine that opposes government regulation beyond the minimum necessary for free enterprise. History has demonstrated that, in its purest form, it is a radical concept. Regulation is needed.*

*Ízzat faire is a whimsical phrase that, while sounding like a foreign language, is really a* word corruption *that simply begs the question, is that fair? We feel that ízzat faire should apply to commerce, regulation, Wall Street, and government at all levels.*

*Who was Adam Smith?*

*Glad you asked. The eighteenth century economist was most famous for his authorship of* The Wealth of Nations, *published in 1776. Born on June 5, 1723 at Kirkcaldy, Scotland, he was a colleague of Ben Franklin, among other notables. His writings illustrated the fact that* free markets *work most effectively and result in the greatest production of goods at the most competitive costs with moderate regulation. He posited that every individual, in seeking to satisfy their own greed within a free society, is led, as though by an* invisible hand, *to procure the greatest good for all. Adam Smith passed on July 17, 1790...but his spirit remains, as Jane will soon learn.*

# Chapter Three

As Jane sorted through the day's mail, she realized that about every other piece was some plea to invest in yet some other mining company, remote project, mutual fund family, or insurance product, or an invitation to some *class* that would allegedly solve all her investment problems. Normally, she might chuckle to herself, but present circumstances only made her feel more unhappy. She found a postcard touting investment classes intriguing and thought *I should call Bryce to learn more. Perhaps I should be less narrow-minded.* For Jane, that was an epiphany!

While opening several more pieces of mail, she came upon an invitation that looked to be trimly engraved in real gold. It was beautiful! Upon opening the envelope, she found that it was an invitation to take a trip on the "Oceans of Investment Opportunity." The departure date was several days out, and mysteriously, the invitation was signed in ink by "S.O.S."

The concept excited Jane as she realized a fragile nexus with her recent past. Could this have something to do with Bryce and Adam Smith? She truly wanted to learn more about their proven concepts but seemed torn between two grand opportunities. She decided to seek Bryce's advice and telephoned him. When she told him about the exquisite invitation she had received and read the context of the invitation, he chuckled knowingly. "That's Adam!" he exclaimed. "Jane, we really do want to take you on an educational cruise that will take you into a world of investing efficiency unlike anything you've ever dreamed of. But, you need to approach this opportunity with an open mind. Adam probably signed the card 'S.O.S.' Am I right?"

"He sure did," Jane retorted. "What do the initials mean?"

"He represents 'S.O.S.,' the 'spirit of success,' in all his endeavors. Adam Smith is like an avatar. He is the embodiment of a bodily manifestation, an incarnation that has been around for a very long time, Jane. Brace yourself because I have to tell you that he wrote a book way back in 1776 entitled *The Wealth of Nations*. Jane, are you still with me?"

"Unbelievable!" screamed Jane.

"Jane, he is actually the father of economic science as we know it today, and frankly, while brilliant, at times he can be really amusing and even mischievous. Adam tinkers at a level that blows my mind. He has hobbies that could result in whole industries. He is developing a power source he calls an 'air engine,' which is a device that converts the energy from compressed air into kinetic energy

# CHAPTER THREE

that can drive any type of machine. He tells me that the concept was very effective in the nineteenth century, powering coalmine locomotives and has been used to power naval torpedoes since 1866. I have to believe him because he was probably an eyewitness back then."

Jane displayed a quizzical look and an unbelieving smile.

Bryce went on. "Jane, I'm not kidding! He also spends time on what he calls a 'water splitting engine' that converts water into hydrogen to provide energy to power machines."

Jane was chuckling now. "Something like the explosive power of *anti-matter* when it collides with matter?"

"I guess," Bryce answered. He went on to explain that Adam also works on solar power and wind turbine technology when he gets bored. "Regardless of his eccentricities, Jane, I respect Adam and have found his counsel continues to be second to none."

Jane was more serious now as she confided, "Bryce, I have had dreams lately about the *spirit of success* and cannot believe all this is suddenly coming together. I recall *The Wealth of Nations* book from college finance and really admire your friend Mr. Adam Smith. Please tell me what the trip on the *oceans of opportunity* involves."

"Adam's apparition has the uncanny ability to compress time. What he wishes to do is have you board our vessel and travel to distant lands while compressing time in an effort to maximize your education in a most interesting fashion while minimizing months of travel on the

## THE WALL STREET CASINO

Oceans of Opportunity. Jane, I can assure you that the trip is worth the effort. Adam has often said that the future is not what it used to be—and he ought to know. I know that he can make you feel more comfortable with your investments and offer insight that can change your investment future and that of your family. We both understand your concern about your mother's illness and your desire to stay near. I can assure you this whole educational adventure will require only three days in real time."

Jane was both relieved and overly excited as she accepted Bryce and Adam's generous offer. "Great! Let's plan to cast off at 8:00 a.m., Tuesday," Bryce commanded.

"Wait! What areas does 'S.O.S.' plan to visit so that I know how to pack?"

"We'll be visiting very profitable land masses and not so profitable land masses to learn about the economies and cultural differences. They will include Africa, China, and Russia, as well as the investment capital of America, New York City. Sound exciting?"

"It certainly does," Jane agreed as she cradled her head in her hands in anticipation of her coming adventure. "But, the trip will cover thousands of miles. Is three days even remotely plausible?" she queried.

"Adam can compress more ideas into fewer words than any person I have ever encountered…and he does the same with time," Bryce assured her.

Tuesday dawned with a sky blushing red at sunrise and Jane was reminded of the seaman's limerick "red sky at night,

## CHAPTER THREE

sailor's delight; red sky in the morning, sailors take warning." How totally appropriate, she thought; as if the stock market activity was not bad enough…apparently, we will be departing in heavy weather. (She was reminded that Wall Street's J. P. Morgan financed the doomed *Titanic*.) She shuddered as she pulled her car into the yacht club parking area.

When she arrived at the dock, she saw that Adam Smith and "Captain" Bryce had readied the yacht and warmed the engines. "Ahoy, mate!" exclaimed Bryce as he stepped onto the dock to help deliver what appeared to him to be a massive amount of Jane's luggage onto the aft deck. Jane was impressed with the appearance of the yacht as the sun cast highlights on the hull, gleaming brightwork, and gunnels' trim. The brightwork indicated the yacht was very well maintained. It appeared to be about eighty feet in length with a beam width of twenty feet, and the name on the stern was *Aquarius*. It was one of the top quality Azimut motor yachts. Bryce was right. It sure was a "bigger boat"! Jane was truly excited.

Aquarius

She could not help but notice how handsome Bryce appeared with his captain's hat and how somehow, Adam Smith looked younger and far less foreboding. "Good morning! How are you?" she queried as she waved to Mr. Smith.

"And good morning to you, young lady!" responded Mr. Smith with a broad smile and a wave of his hand.

Bryce approached Jane and gave her a strong hug and a kiss on the left cheek. "Glad to see you, Jane! It's a beautiful day, and this is going to be a great voyage!" Bryce said, as they both passed her luggage into the salon.

Jane's birthday was January 25. She thought it an unusual coincidence that the vessel's name was *Aquarius*, her astrological sign. She mentioned the coincidence to Mr. Smith. He explained that because she was born under the Aquarius zodiac sign, she was therefore friendly, honest, and loyal. He said that Jane was a zesty person that takes pride in the fact that she is unique...even if she is a disbeliever in the more efficient passive investment concept. Jane had to chuckle at Adam's candor. He explained that the zodiac symbol is the Water Bearer. The act of pouring water is representative of Aquarius dispensing investment truths to the world, he said. He explained that the name on the stern was no accident. He said that both he and Bryce considered their life's goal to be that of dispensing investment truths. Jane had just received lesson number one.

Bryce gave the command to Mr. Smith to cast off. The vessel moved astern and with Bristol elegance, sailed to port following the channel into Lake Erie, destined to arrive in compressed time at Cape Town, South Africa, in almost no time at all. Interestingly, Jane hoped that the travel time would not be too compressed because she wished to spend some time with Bryce. Of course, she also welcomed

## CHAPTER THREE

the presence of Mr. Smith and hoped that he would enlighten her with what he and Bryce had referred to as "passive investing" and "investment efficiency."

It seemed only minutes before they reached the broad expanse of Lake Erie. Bryce remained vigilant, piloting the vessel from the bridge while Adam Smith invited Jane's questions. "Mr. Smith, I want to thank you for taking the time to visit with me regarding my investment dilemma. I am afraid I have probably made every investment error that any investor could possibly commit. I understand and respect the fact that you're a fine looking eighteenth century apparition. I'll bet you can enlighten me from the very beginning of investment history."

"Yes, Jane, I have been around a good while. Being this old is both a blessing and a curse. I am blessed in that I sleep more soundly now. Unfortunately, that usually takes place in the afternoon! I feel even older when touring museums only to find that I am saying to myself, 'I remember these.'"

"Oh, stop," Jane said with a smile.

"No. It's true, Jane. I have now found that I can avoid wrinkles by simply removing my glasses when I walk past the mirror."

"Oh, yes, that works for all of us, Mr. Smith," Jane chuckled.

"Jane, please call me Adam and realize that I am here in your presence as well as in the minds of thousands as we speak. Apparitions have that ability! I have often said that history is not what it used to be. By that, I mean that we live in a time of accelerated technological progress. Jane, if you feel that what you are going through is exciting for you, please try to envision how exciting my effort today is for me. To be here now and be able to recognize the important impact my *Wealth of Nations* book has had on millions of investors is truly rewarding.

"Yes, I told Bryce that I studied your wonderful book in college. I can't imagine how proud you must be today! But, Adam, Bryce told me about your scientific hobbies. I was particularly intrigued by what he called an air engine. How could such a device be possible?" Jane inquired.

"Aye. Remember the 1937 classic written by Napoleon Hill entitled *Think and Grow Rich!* As I recall, Mr. Hill stated that whatever man can conceive…and believe, can be achieved. Certainly, Thomas Savery must have believed that to be so when he invented the first steam engine. That invention resulted in the era of piston steam engines that gave way now to the turbine steam engines and even nuclear powered heat that creates steam today. In the 1900s, the "Stirling engine" utilized a hot air side and a cold air side to drive a piston. I intend to employ concentrated solar rays on one side of multiple pistons and cryogenic cold to the other side. Jane, I think we abandoned the efficiency of air engines when J. Faraday developed *direct current* , which led to William Sturgeon's creation of the first electric motor in 1832. That invention led to the revolutionary automobile *starter motor* in 1911.

# CHAPTER THREE

"Those events made the Model T Ford, with its gasoline combustion engine, practical at a time when gasoline was very economical. That transition occurred in the early 1900s. Then, Nicholas Otto developed the four-stroke engine, which is still being used today. The innovation that most fascinates me regarding the air engine is actually the creation by Felix Wankel. He invented the *rotary engine*, which actually utilizes a rotor rather than pistons.

"Jane, this is probably more than you want to know, but the science of thermodynamics was actually formalized way back in 1824 when a brilliant scientist named Sadi Carnot wrote a book entitled *Reflections on the Motive Power of Fire*. In fact, Zero Pollution Motors in Brignoles, France, recently introduced its e.Volution air powered auto in Johannesburg, South Africa, at the Auto Africa Expo Show. I think they expect the car will go on sale in South Africa in 2002."

"Fascinating," said Jane. "Please go on."

"It seems to me, Jane, that the solution to the concerns surrounding air pollution and the high cost of fuel in the future might be alleviated through the application of *compressed air motors* if we can develop a non-polluting, universal means of compressing the air to drive the motors. Wind turbines could supply the electricity, and *gas stations* would become clean, green *air stations*. Though many of the advantages are obvious, some are not so apparent. The compressed air motor exhaust would actually be cold air, which could be captured to condition air in the passenger cabin. A heat exchanger could also convert the air to warmer air during cold months in order to keep the passengers comfortable. While there is much research to be done in these areas, it would appear that these concepts do offer promise. But now, let's spend some time on the history that surrounds *investments* so that you might feel a bit more comfortable.

"Perhaps we should begin our futuristic examination of investing by explaining how it is that mutual fund investors of the future frequently miss out on fully 78% of a fund's positive progress. I know that it seems impossible, but it is true! Passive investment legend John Bogle presented a detailed study in his book entitled *The Little Book of Common Sense Investing*.

**Profit on Initial Investment of $10,000, 1980–2005**

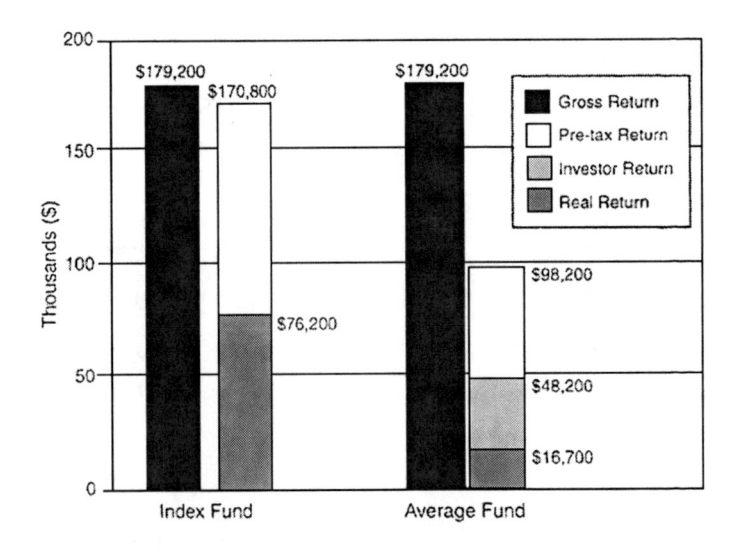

| | Index Fund | Average Fund |
|---|---|---|
| Gross Return | $179,200 | $179,200 |
| Pre-tax Return | $170,800 | $98,200 |
| Investor Return | $76,200 | $48,200 |
| Real Return | | $16,700 |

Source: "The Little Book of Common Sense Investing" by John C. Bogle

# CHAPTER THREE

"Mr. Bogle stated that during the past 25 years, while the stock market index fund was providing an annual return of 12.3 percent and the average equity fund was earning an annual return of 10 percent, the average fund investor was earning only 7.3 percent a year. Compounded over the entire period, a 2.5 percent interior fund expense was actually huge. The bar chart illustrates that $10,000 invested in the index fund grew to $170,800 while, in the average equity fund, growth was only $98,200,- just 57 percent of the index fund growth. Note that the *after tax* compound return earned by the average fund investor tumbled to $48,200,- 28 percent of the simple index fund!

We must then consider inflation, which drops the real index fund investor return to 9 percent and the average fund investor to only 4 percent. On a compound basis, $76,200 of real investor value for the index fund compared to $16,700 for the average fund investor equals only 22 percent of the potential growth. Iżzat faire?

Adam reached behind the couch, produced a well-worn leather binder, and showed Jane the bar graph that illuminated the glaring benefit of *passively* managed *index funds* relative to the far less efficient *actively managed* retail stock funds. (Jane, of course, marveled at the fact that Adam could produce accurate projections through 2005!)

# ROBERT KNEISLEY
# NOTES

# CHAPTER THREE

# Author's Comment

*Not so long ago, one of the most outstanding football players, Walter Gibbs of the Green Bay Packers, died in an accident. Coach Vince Lombardi tells the story of the first time this great success entered the locker room as a rookie. Mr. Lombardi welcomed the new recruits by presenting a football and announcing, "Gentlemen, this is a football." "Not so fast!" remarked Mr. Gibbs.*

*Like Mr. Lombardi, investors frequently move faster on a hot tip than they should. Remember, folks like to tell you about their winners but frequently dismiss the many losers. We always advise clients who wish to follow the next tip to do so on paper ONLY...and then at least ten times. More often than not, those clients who follow the paper trades suffer paper losses of no consequence and learn a valuable lesson. The same approach works well when educating children or grandchildren.*

*Mr. Gibb's comment may have been helpful to those who fell into the sub-prime mess of 2007. The Center for Economic and Policy Research estimates that declining home prices since mid-2006 have slashed more than $4 trillion in real housing wealth. (That is more than $50,000 for every homeowner in the country!)*

**Don't go "gaga" over the next "go-go" investment vehicle.**

*Auction rate securities are tied to mortgage securities, and they represent about $330 billion held by investors in a market that quite literally dried up due to the credit crunch created by the real estate bubble. Unfortunately, the Wall Street firms that created the auction rate securities concept left their own sales people hard pressed to explain away the fact that thousands of investors could not liquidate*

# THE WALL STREET CASINO

*their auction rate securities since February, 2008. They finally paid investors par value, plus interest, in August 2008 according to Investment News.*

*By mid-September, the government had to bail out Fannie Mae and Freddie Mac, giant Merrill Lynch was bought out by Bank of America, and Lehman Brothers was in Chapter 11 bankruptcy. Apparently, Wall Street had gone "gaga"...and all investors paid the price!*

# Chapter Four

"I am very comfortable knowing that Captain Bryce is in control up on the bridge. We now have some time to go back in history and recount what went before in an effort to establish a foundation for sensible investment strategies for today," Adam said as he took a seat on the sofa directly across from Jane in the luxurious salon. Suddenly, Jane noted that the windows behind him resembled the rapidly moving horizontal blur of a television screen with no input signal. It was as she might imagine space travel!

Aquarius's Main Salon

The apparition leaned back on the sofa, placed both hands behind his head, and said, "Roundly speaking,

## THE WALL STREET CASINO

Jane, I think it's safe to say that today technology and life both come at us much faster than in my day. Back then, it took many days to transport information from one town to another. But, to fully grasp the concept I am referring to we would have to go back to the Stone Age some two million years before Christ. To say that those were difficult times is to jest.

"It actually took a million years before the discovery of fire! That discovery, of course, brought the cave dwellers to the Metals Age a million years before Christ. History accelerated a bit after that because the Agricultural Age, 8,000 years before Christ, required only 992,000 years after the Metals Age to appear.

"That gave birth to the first permanent towns and farming and then, the Renaissance Age occurred in 1450 A.D. Only 9,450 years had passed," he said with a chuckle. "And that gave us, as you may recall, the printing press and the beginnings of industrialized society which appeared in 1700 A.D.

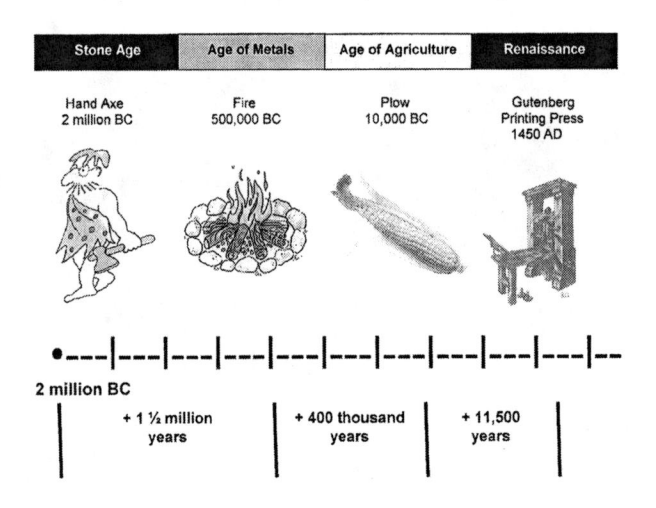

| Stone Age | Age of Metals | Age of Agriculture | Renaissance |
|---|---|---|---|
| Hand Axe<br>2 million BC | Fire<br>500,000 BC | Plow<br>10,000 BC | Gutenberg<br>Printing Press<br>1450 AD |

●---|---|---|---|---|---|---|---|---|--

2 million BC      + 1 ½ million years     + 400 thousand years     + 11,500 years

## CHAPTER FOUR

Mind you, Jane, only 250 years had passed to bring us to the factory system and 125 years thereafter to the Transportation Age in 1825 A.D. It was at this time that the first railway train appeared and then things really accelerated. As recently as 1957, the first Earth satellite appeared. Only 132 years had passed since the Transportation Age. Then, a scant 14 years later, the Information Age gave way to the *Computer Age* in 1971. The first microprocessor was born that year. Jane, today business plans that not so long ago were ten-year and five-year plans have now been compressed, much like our trip, to only a matter of months. While the result is very positive for industrialized, high technology nations, the time compression is highly confusing to investors."

Now laughing with gusto, Mr. Smith said, "I believe it was Mark Twain who said, and I'll quote here: 'October is one of the peculiarly dangerous months in which to speculate in stocks. The others are July, January, September, April, November, May, March, June, December, Au-

| Industrial Age | Information Age | Knowledge Age |
|---|---|---|
| Steam Engine + Assembly Line 1769 AD | Computer Chip 1958 AD | Age of Technology 1990 AD |

--|---|---|---|---|---|---•---|

+ 319 years   + 189 years   Birth of Christ
                            + 32 years

Source: Indicator Advisory Research/Oxford Encyclopedia & www.orisonarm.com

55

gust and February!' Jane, I believe Mr. Twain was a realist when he described such speculation.

"Jane, it is sad that investors do not hold their mutual fund investments for longer periods of time in order to reap the benefits of doing so. While the stock market's real rate of return has been remarkably steady over long periods, the rate has been subject to considerable variation from year to year and these wide variations tend to decline sharply over time." Adam presented the bar chart below that shows that a one-year standard deviation (a measure of volatility) of 18.1% drops by more than half, to 7.5%, over just five years. It is reduced to only 4.4% over ten years. The volatility continues to decrease until it reaches only 1% over an investment lifetime of fifty years with an upper

**Range of Stock Market Annual Returns**

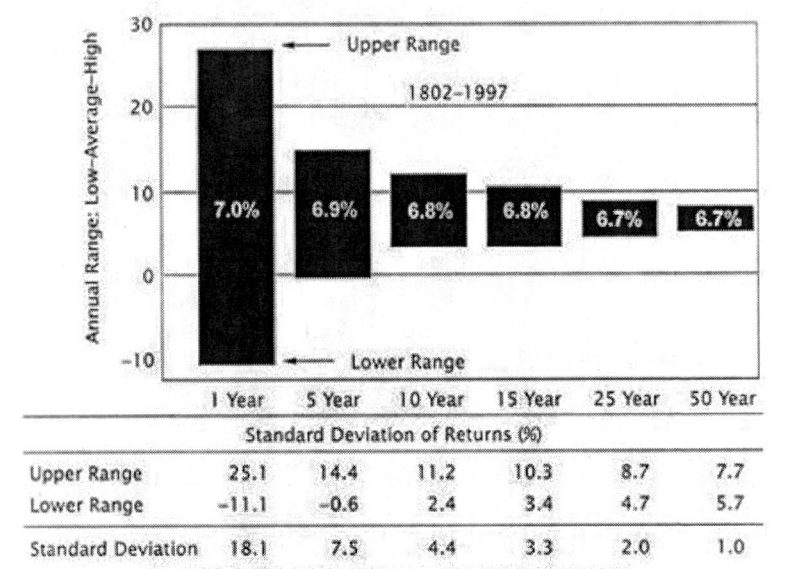

1802-1997

| | 1 Year | 5 Year | 10 Year | 15 Year | 25 Year | 50 Year |
|---|---|---|---|---|---|---|
| | 7.0% | 6.9% | 6.8% | 6.8% | 6.7% | 6.7% |
| Standard Deviation of Returns (%) | | | | | | |
| Upper Range | 25.1 | 14.4 | 11.2 | 10.3 | 8.7 | 7.7 |
| Lower Range | -11.1 | -0.6 | 2.4 | 3.4 | 4.7 | 5.7 |
| Standard Deviation | 18.1 | 7.5 | 4.4 | 3.3 | 2.0 | 1.0 |

Source: John C. Bogle from: "Common Sense on Mutual Funds: New Imperatives for the Intelligent Investor"

## CHAPTER FOUR

range of return equaling 7.7% and a lower range of 5.7%. "So, the longer the time horizon is, the less the variability in average annual returns. Foundations and endowments at our colleges and universities, as well as other durable institutions, have been highly successful because they essentially have unlimited time horizons.

"Time is required because history has demonstrated that <u>no one</u> is capable of predicting the future consistently in spite of the thousands of *analysts* that purport to do so. A very broad base of knowledge exists in support of the theory that *free markets* work. Jane, do you remember Archimedes? As I recall, he was the brilliant fellow that reasoned that given a lever long enough and strong enough, he could lift the world. I believe that to be so. Much more recently, Albert Einstein indicated that humankind's most powerful discovery is *compound interest*. Both of those academic presumptions are accurate.

"If we look at the range of rolling average returns on stocks, bonds, and cash over any 20-year period, we find that the volatility, that is to say the movement up and down, is dramatically reduced to the point where losses are nonexistent in the twentieth year. What does this tell us? Well, simply that long-term investing, like Archimedes' lever, works. However, my observation today is that the average growth *retail* mutual fund investor holds the investment for only a few years. Curious, isn't it?

"What is said in my book is that every individual in pursuing his own good is led, as if by an invisible hand, to achieve the best for all. As I recall, I wrote then that 'When the law does not enforce the performance of contracts, it puts all borrowers nearly upon the same footing as bankrupts or people of doubtful credit in better regulated countries.' That statement applies to investment as well, and it has not changed, even with the advent of increased regulation and accelerated technology. Our future, of course, has been dynamically altered. Today, Jane, there is more *random noise* in media of every sort than the average investor can logically absorb. If you have studied history, you will understand that back in my day we had charlatans of every ilk. While history may not repeat itself, it does echo. Technology today makes it possible for all types of powerful financial services and insurance corporations to spend billions of dollars convincing us of their virtuous ability to not only read the future but also portend which enterprises stand to benefit the most. Balderdash! That is why we must have consistent government guidelines supporting free markets." He produced the mountain chart on page 59 and pointed out the positive performance accomplished by investors in spite of Wall Street's interference.

"The wonder of compound interest that Professor Einstein referred to exists in the expanse of time. Jane, if your friend the stockbroker had to exist financially in an environment where people held their investments long-term, he and his industry would not be nearly as profitable. You need to think about that.

"Furthermore, I would ask you to contemplate why

# CHAPTER FOUR

**Cumulative Returns on U.S. Financial Assets (December 31, 1871, to December 31, 1992)**

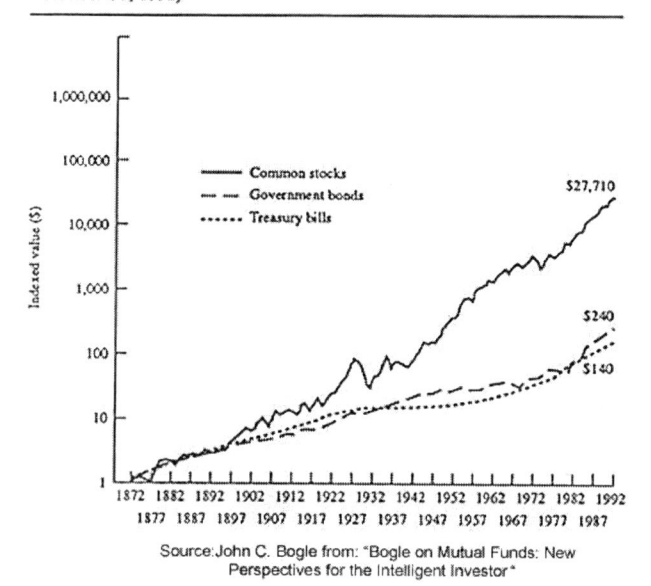

[Chart showing indexed value ($) from 1872 to 1992, with Common stocks reaching $27,710, Government bonds at $240, and Treasury bills at $140]

Source: John C. Bogle from: "Bogle on Mutual Funds: New Perspectives for the Intelligent Investor"

mutual fund *families* have one hundred, two hundred, three hundred, four hundred, or more mutual funds in the family. Let's be honest, Jane, if they could truly foresee the future—if they could truly project the winning stocks—if they could truly know when to buy, hold, and sell those stocks, how many funds would they need in their family?"

Jane looked puzzled. She exhibited a deep frown as she came to the realization that not more than a few hundred funds of each style would solve every growth investor's problem in such a stratified environment—this, instead of the eight thousand plus existing today! Adam proceeded to explain *determination and probability* as a science. It was the phenomenon involving the "law of large numbers," he said. Out of the hundreds of funds, the sponsor is bound by the rule to experience a few that, by pure coincidence, will outperform the others. And, he asked, "Which funds would you imagine the fund sponsor might promote next year?" Mr. Smith laughed heartily as he realized that Jane comprehended the concept.

Adam went on to explain how millions of investors rely upon the Morningstar rankings, which are traditionally measured with one- to five-star symbols. He assured Jane that any ranking with five stars meant that the entity, whether it is a restaurant, hotel, or mutual fund, was a *primo* discovery. He suggested that the mutual fund sponsors frequently operate a fund for up to three years before introducing the fund to Morningstar for their rating. This, he contended, was because Morningstar would not track a fund and give it a star rating until it has been in existence for three years. This fact allows the fund sponsor to introduce only successful funds. "Rather self-serving wouldn't you say, Jane?"

"I should say so," Jane agreed. She felt assured of the accuracy of Mr. Smith's brief comments and, looking at her wristwatch, was surprised to note that only a minute or two had passed. She marveled at this unique time compression experience and wondered how far they had traveled.

"Land ho!" bellowed the salon intercom from the bridge. The captain of the *Aquarius* announced that he had sighted South Africa and would soon disembark at Cape Town.

Jane was very impressed with the eloquence of Mr. Smith's observations, and she welcomed the opportunity to visit with Bryce. She thanked Adam for his insight as she reached in her purse for her passport. Bryce and Mr. Smith

## CHAPTER FOUR

had made all the arrangements to assure an enjoyable visit in Cape Town. They had also invited a local finance professor to join them for lunch.

Jane appreciated the innate beauty of the lush shoreline as they approached the Cape. She was surprised, however, by the great size of the major seaport. Bryce and Mr. Smith secured *Aquarius* to the dock. Captain Bryce hailed a cab, which, to Jane's dismay, turned out to be a shabby mechanical conveyance with a soiled interior. She noted, however, that they passed some brand new, shiny cabs on the highway. As they traveled, Mr. Smith explained that Cape Town possessed a capitalist infrastructure because of its earlier links to the British Empire. Financial services appeared in the 1840s and 1850s at a time when colonial shopkeepers, traders, and financiers, as well as the agricultural industry nurtured commerce. Cape Town grew to more than 30,000 people by 1950. Mr. Smith explained that the British government granted settlers a *representative government* in 1853 and allowed some Africans to vote in about 1872. Unfortunately, he stated that these nominal privileges were reduced and finally abolished outright in 1936.

Mr. Smith seemed saddened as he pointed out that European missionaries and their African understudies attempted to Christianize indigenous communities in the 1820s. Paralleling this effort, they attempted to introduce the populace to European manufactured goods. Their efforts, however, undermined African world views and contributed to the de-

## THE WALL STREET CASINO

struction of traditional African communities. This intrusion on the African *free markets* led to extreme difficulty on the part of Africans to obtain capital. The results were political and legal discrimination that resulted in driving many South African entrepreneurs out of business.

Mr. Smith pointed out that the early South African economy was narrowly based on wine and wool and was not very prosperous. (Australia became the region's biggest producer of wool in 1855.) Around 1870, the most potentially rewarding commodities were diamonds, which were discovered in the Vaal Valley, and gold found in the Tati Valley and in the northern and eastern Transvaal.

Shortly, the threesome arrived at Simon's Town, which most might recognize as the Cape of Good Hope. Bryce had selected Bertha's, a seaside, upscale restaurant for their luncheon and had invited a Professor Maboto to join them. The beautifully appointed restaurant offered an abundant view of the Atlantic Ocean and bustling seashore. Before ordering their entrée, they enjoyed a casual cocktail, and Bryce and Jane engaged in conversation with hands clasped under the table. Mr. Smith, meanwhile, explained their interest in visiting with anyone that the receptionist might know that

Bertha's Restaurant

## CHAPTER FOUR

would help them better understand the financial circumstances and economy of Cape Town and South Africa. The receptionist was very accommodating, and she escorted Mr. Malcolm Jacobs to Mr. Smith, introducing Mr. Jacobs to all as a local historian and community leader. Since Mr. Jacobs was unaccompanied, Mr. Smith invited him to join his threesome. Mr. Jacobs graciously accepted, and they chatted over cocktails.

Cape Town, South Africa

Upon questioning, Mr. Jacobs explained that while capitalism was paramount in their economy, the country was still recovering from British Rule. He stated that most slaves, by decree of the local magistrate, were freed in 1838. Mr. Jacobs pointed out that the growth of capitalism in South Africa was a positive trend. He said that the diamond industry provided fundamental support for the economy. Deeper discussion followed between Mr. Jacobs and Mr. Smith regarding *free markets*, and Mr. Jacobs reinforced Mr. Smith's statement that free markets are best for a country's economy and for the citizens of the country.

"Bryce! Adam!" exclaimed Professor Maboto as he strode toward them at a fast pace. "Welcome to Africa! It is great to see you both again…and I look forward to your introduction to the beautiful lady." Bryce and Adam rose to greet the professor.

"Great to be here, Professor. How have you been?" asked Bryce as he shook hands with the professor.

"Wonderful! It is always a pleasure to visit with you and Adam. And who is this charming young lady?"

"Professor, we would like you to meet an old college friend of mine, Jane Cromwell. And, Professor, this is Mr. Jacobs, a local historian and community leader. The professor is the renowned financial writer and leading professor of finance at the university here in Africa, Professor Maboto. Please have a seat Professor," Bryce said as he gestured toward a fifth chair at the table. "We are delighted that you could join us. We are on another of our *excursions* and have brought Jane with us in order to enable her to better understand financial developments in Africa in general and the different financial cultures throughout the world. Perhaps you would be kind enough to give us a brief snapshot concerning Africa and the degree that capitalism might be creeping into the economic culture of this vast land?"

"Bryce, you know that nothing pleases me more than expounding on what progress we find here in Africa, and I am privileged to be able to discuss these matters with Jane and Mr. Jacobs as well. Jane, where would you like me to start?"

"Wherever you like, Professor. I am all ears!" Jane responded.

"Well then, let us start with some current history so that you have a strong footing as to our limited progress in the

# CHAPTER FOUR

last few decades. I am sorry to say that Africa is a very poor region and is afflicted with a devastating disease called AIDS and a very weak, even fragmented, economy. Adam, Africa is perhaps the last frontier for capitalistic growth and is a fine example of your belief that controlled greed is the best approach to economic development. We are finally seeing some of that here in Africa. We continue, however, to suffer from fits of growth and recession.

Mozambique fought for independence from Portugal and won it in 1975. Sadly, millions of citizens lost their lives or were crippled or displaced. Jane, Adam and Bryce would explain to you that our grand continent supports about one seventh of the world's population and occupies approximately 25% of the world's land. On the one hand, we are blessed with this great land...but it is not fertile. We desperately require fertilizer, which is in extremely short supply. Investment capital is only trickling into Africa. I pray only that the trickle will grow into rivers in the years ahead. It really should, based upon the abundance of natural resources our country possesses." The professor seemed to bow his head in prayer for a brief moment.

Then, Professor Maboto went on to explain the history of racial inequality and the efforts to overcome that problem. He pointed out that the apartheid system resulted in tremendous inequality of education for natives of his country until the multiracial election in 1994. The professor frowned as he looked deeply into Adam's eyes. "Adam, I am very concerned that the other face of greed might result in a slowdown of the growth in both the African economy as well as that of the United States. It appears to me that the financial services industry has successfully educated the investing populace in a way that not only is detrimental, but is being exported to Africa and throughout the globe."

# CHAPTER FOUR

# Notes

**ROBERT KNEISLEY**

## Author's Comment

*It would seem that the wisdom of the apparition of Mr. Smith transcends centuries. He had selected Africa as their first destination. He did so because Africa, of course, is the least wealthy continent on the planet—this, in spite of the fact that over 600 billion dollars in foreign aid has flowed into the region since 1960! Mr. Smith is endeavoring to indicate to Jane that his earlier statement concerning personal greed represents the very foundation of economic development in this poorest of areas. In fact, Africa might well be the investment world's final global frontier. We can only hope that worldwide investment will spur the economy and improve the extremely harsh living conditions on this huge continent. I think Mr. Smith and Bryce have arranged to focus on many of these issues.*

### "Maniacal Math" and the Short-term Investor Phenomenon

Mr. John C. Bogle is the founder and former CEO of the Vanguard Mutual Fund Group. I had the pleasure of meeting Mr. Bogle in New York many years ago while I was employed with a leading Wall Street brokerage firm. I have admired Mr. Bogle and his investment brilliance for many decades. His Bogle Research Group has been gracious in their assistance with research for this book.

In Mr. Bogle's recent book entitled The Little Book of Common Sense Investing, he eloquently addresses "yesterday's winners and tomorrow's losers" in chapter nine. Mr. Bogle points out the fact that most mutual fund investors focus on exciting short-term performance rather than sustained long-term performance... to their detriment. Again, I feel that the focus on short-term performance is often because they are receiving a recommendation based upon a recent track record espoused by a retail salesperson.

# CHAPTER FOUR

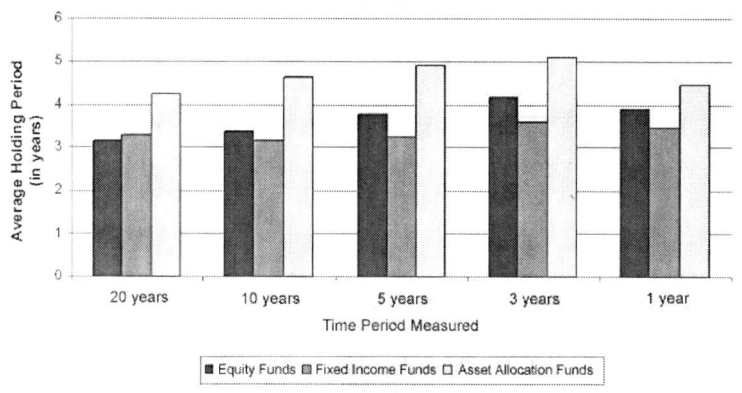

**Investor Holding Periods
for the Periods Ending 12/31/07
Time Period: 1/88-12/07**

[Bar chart showing Average Holding Period (in years) versus Time Period Measured (20 years, 10 years, 5 years, 3 years, 1 year) for Equity Funds, Fixed Income Funds, and Asset Allocation Funds]

Source: DALBAR 2008 QAIB Study

Mr. Bogle states that 95% of investor dollars are invested in funds rated 4 or 5 by Morningstar. The "star ratings" are based on a composite of a mutual fund's performance over three-, five-, and ten-year periods. The "star" process creates a built-in bias in favor of short-term performance.

Sadly, the short-term orientation of fund investors works the worst in strong bull markets. Mr. Bogle's research indicates that the top ten performers among the 851 equity funds operating during the "new economy" market bubble of 1997–1999 generated an average return of 55% per year during that exciting bull market blow-off. The cumulative return was 279% for the full three years!

It is critical for investors to note that when the bubble burst the next three years through 2002 found _every one_ of those top ten funds plummeting into the bottom ranked sixty funds. Not a single fund in the original top ten ranked higher than 790! Fund number 9 during the bull market was actually last, –851 on the downside. Investors should surely avoid their myopic focus on short-term performance.

# THE WALL STREET CASINO

## Three Examples of "Maniacal Math":

*"I bought the car on the installment plan because I need the tax write-off."*

*"Last year, my fund was up 30%. This year, I'm down 20%, so I'm still up 10%, right?"*

*"I used my 401(k) debit card because it's so convenient to access my capital gains."*

These quotations from otherwise intelligent investors have puzzled me over the years. Buying on the installment plan does indeed give us a tax write-off. However, if we are in the 30% marginal tax bracket, the write-off amounts to thirty cents of every dollar. Why do these borrowers continue to throw away seventy cents?

In the second case, we should do the arithmetic. If we had invested $100, and it grew 30%, we, of course, would have $130. If we then have a loss of 20%, that percentage applies to the total $130, correct? Of course, it does. That amount would be $26. If we deduct the $26 from our $130, we find that we have only a 4% gain. If our account is a taxable account, and we apply taxes and inflation, more than likely, we are underwater.

The only other quick way we can get underwater in our retirement planning is to use a debit card to access our 401(k). Such loans grew from $6 billion to $31 billion (inflation-adjusted dollars) in the second half of 2004. Remember, disturbing the compounding curve early in the compounding cycle can amount to thousands of dollars fifteen to twenty years distant. My recommendation would be to never use a debit card and never borrow from your 401(k).

Let's read on.

# Chapter Five

The Professor surely had everyone's attention at this point. Bryce suggested that the professor discuss specific examples, as he understood them. Smiling, the professor said, "Let's start at the beginning so that Mr. Jacobs and Jane will understand my concerns about the current trend and later, the advantages proven by academia with regard to *passive investing* and asset-class index funds. First, a brief lesson in American history would start with the *stockjobbers* that frequented the saloons in an area known as New Netherlands and New Amsterdam in about 1624 in North America. You may recall that Peter Minuit negotiated the purchase of Manhattan Island from the Indians for approximately $24 in trinkets. Adam, that was long before your time; however, it does show the power of greed. As I recall, that was in about 1626.

"Perhaps, you remember that in the mid-1600s, the British seized New Netherlands and New Amsterdam and renamed the territory after the Duke of York—hence, the name New York. Actually, the fence that was converted to a fortified stockade in 1653 was designed to prevent the British from a land attack and the very footprint of that fence is what we know today as Wall Street. Adam, it was 1776 when you wrote *The Wealth of Nations*, which changed the course of history in a very positive way. Would you grace us with your impression of early American history going forward?"

"Nothing would delight me more!" Adam rested his chin on his left hand as he said thoughtfully, "Well, the War of 1812 ensued at about the same time the New York Stock Board was established, and as I recall, the first mutual fund was created for widows in 1815. The Scots established the fund and not very creatively, I feel, christened it the 'Widow's Fund' since it was founded to provide for widows whose spouses were lost at sea. In about 1863, the New York Stock Board name was revised to the New York Stock Exchange because so much Spanish currency was being *exchanged* at that time. Interestingly, some of that currency included *pieces of eight*, which were milled dollar coins that could be divided into eighths with a hammer and chisel." Adam smiled with a chuckle as he explained that it was for this reason that United States securities were quoted in *eighths* until decimal pricing came into effect in the year 2000.

Pieces of Eight

# CHAPTER FIVE

He pointed out that investment today is a global effort but still not nearly as efficient as it could be. Therein lies the reason for global portfolio diversification in one's investing, coupled with proper asset allocation and the need to rebalance one's portfolio periodically in order to maintain the proper mix between fixed income and growth investments.

"As I recall, it was May 1, 1975... affectionately referred to as 'May Day' by the stockjobbers of the day. May Day was in fact the result of computerization of the then new NASDAQ electronic trading system, which included *flexible* commissions. I think that took place in about 1971 and forced the major brokerages to re-evaluate their position, which resulted in *negotiated commissions*. The lower commissions saw institutional commission income to the major brokerages fall by about 40%. Professor, I think this is about the time that you would like to begin your dissertation as to what happened after that huge revenue decline."

"Indeed!" remarked the professor as he placed both hands palms down on the table and flashed a wry smile. "That is where history really got interesting! That was also near the time when adjustable rate mortgages were introduced by the banking powers. Frankly, I was astounded that America's consumers accepted such a brazen attempt on the part of the bankers to off-load the majority of risk of interest rate fluctuations onto the shoulders of the mortgage debtor. I was further surprised that the U.S. Treasury

Department and Federal Reserve would permit such an arrangement. Adjustable rate mortgages are an invitation to more liberalized control of the mortgage market, and they will lead to no good.

"But, let us go back now to the brokerage industry. Be aware that years ago, in the 1940s, mutual fund managers held individual stocks in their growth funds for longer than five years. That is a desirable holding period since mutual funds are supposed to be *long-term* investments, are they not? Of course, they were, and still should be. In the 1970s, that rate began to rise dramatically until today, I must sadly report that internal stock turnover rates have risen from 65% in 1978 to a dramatic 110.3% in 2007 according to Morningstar research.

"Frankly, it frightens me to think that while investors claim to be investing for the long haul, their retail mutual fund managers are reaping extravagant benefits by *churning* stocks within the mutual funds. And be aware Jane and Mr. Jacobs, that this churning creates brokerage *clearing fees* (*commissions* to the average investor). Even Morningstar has estimated that clearing costs add approximately 1½% to 3% to the standard *expense ratio* that averaged about 1.46% in 2007 on growth retail mutual funds. This is in addition to the 4% to 10% upfront commissions that are paid to the brokerage firms. We must add to that the cost of the average <u>internal</u> turnover rate of securities within the equity mutual fund. Such internal trading activity can also create significant capital gains taxes for investors holding

# CHAPTER FIVE

the mutual fund in a taxable account—this, even if the value of the fund has dropped! My friends, this trend is very unhealthy, and I'm afraid these inefficiencies are being exported all over the world."

Bryce was shaking his head in agreement throughout much of the professor's dissertation. Now he felt compelled to carry the conversation regarding the inefficiencies of Wall Street a step further. "Professor, you could not be more correct! It is worth pointing out to our friends that other corollary disadvantages that impact investors are worth discussing. Unsuspecting investors are simply not aware of many things.

"Firstly, when they visit a retail broker/dealer or *brokerage house*, they will normally get that single firm's corporate opinion and will be limited to captive products in all too many instances. Even the sales representatives are unaware of the system the brokerage community employs to place product. Many are unaware of the inborn disadvantages of proprietary products. Many are completely unaware of the fact that mutual funds issuers collect *marketing fees* from brokerages in order for the brokerage company to provide 'shelf space' to market the product.

"Furthermore, since corporate policy rules, there will always appear a constancy of strategic selection that is passed along to the sales staff. Even the sales people may well have somewhat misleading titles such as 'investment counselor', 'investment executive', 'account executive,' or 'financial planner,' rather than simply the *stockbroker* that they actually are. Brokerage management should be more transparent in their dealings with the public by allowing their sales staff to communicate openly with the media and the public—a desirable policy not now in force.

"In 1986, Brinson, Hood, and Beebower studied ninety-one pension plans from the period 1973–1985. They proved the total failure of active management conclusively in 1991. This chart indicates that 91.5% of portfolio performance derives from asset allocation. Market timing accounts for only 1.8%; security selection, only 4.6%. Then, it follows that we must examine how we can proceed to build a successful portfolio to gain a comfortable retirement. It is, after all, your retirement—plan to arrive in style!

Asset Allocation 91.5%
Market Timing 1.8%
Security Selection 4.6%
Other Factors 2.1%

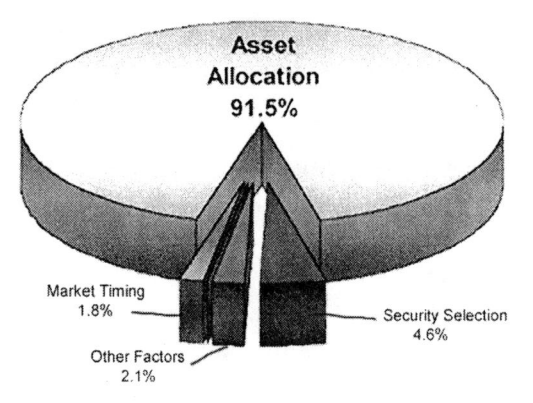

Brinson Beebower Study

Source: Financial Analysts Journal, 1991

"Your advisor is gambling with your investment if they recommend investment decisions that depend upon:

- Track Record Investing
- Market Timing
- Stock Picking

# CHAPTER FIVE

"I say this since it has been proven that track record investing does not work. Studies have shown that outperforming funds throughout history are much like shooting stars. Top performers fall from grace because of poor performance because there is no continuity of short-term performance in the markets. And, regardless of what Wall Street analysts might tell you, no one can predict the future. The second item, market timing, has been disproved through studies that have shown that less than 2% of a portfolio's performance can be achieved through market timing. (Please refer to the pie chart above.) While the last item, stock picking, can be successful around the margins of the overall market, it defies the truism that markets are *efficient*. And, that gets into the whole academic area of the Efficient Market Hypothesis, the Capital Asset Pricing Model, and the diligent research that has been accomplished over the years by the Finance Department at the University of Chicago. Professor, were you aware that the University of Chicago Finance Department has, over the years, garnered twenty-two Nobel laureates in the area of finance alone?"

"That is an impressive fact, Bryce. I would be remiss if I didn't point out to Jane and Mr. Jacobs that what Adam and Bryce do professionally is without question the most efficient approach an investor should employ. I say this because <u>independent</u> advice offers so many necessary advantages to accomplish efficient investing for the investor. And yet, because of the billons of dollars spent annually on advertising by the retail mutual fund companies and the retail brokerage houses, most investors fail. As independent, licensed advisors, Bryce and Adam are not shackled, so they can provide independent research. Doing so results in many premium services, along with the ability to *upgrade* the portfolio or switch as technology dictates as needed to serve the client better over the long haul. Their independent research provides due diligence on many global strategies and unlimited global products and services. I know of no licensed investment advisor that accepts *marketing fees* to place *product* as do the brokerage firms. I would strongly recommend that investors seek out fee-only advisors such as Adam and Bryce because that concept brings synergy to the client/advisor relationship. I think it is important that the advisor be on the *same side of the desk* with the client.

"Be assured further that Bryce and Adam fully *disclose all fees,* including *hidden fees*, unlike their Wall Street counterparts. In addition, there are no commission fees and all fees are <u>tax deductible</u>. Larger investors will also appreciate the fact that these advisors offer *quantity discounts* for larger investments. Jane, these are not like *break points* that represent lower commission fees on retail mutual funds. Rather, these discounts represent lower fees <u>across the board</u> for the larger investor. That is a very significant difference.

"Remember, my friends, it is not how much you earn, it is how much you keep! Which brings me to the impor-

## CHAPTER FIVE

tant topic of *market impact* as it applies to retail mutual funds. The recent declining global stock market is a glowing example that will help me illustrate this point. Given the fact that all investors are driven by fear and greed, it has been proven that in rising markets, investors will commit funds and in declining markets, investors, in fact, do extract funds from the market.

"This fear-driven extraction process involves a telephone call, email, or written directive to the mutual fund manager requesting that she sell the client's holdings. That request, regardless of how it's delivered, forces the mutual fund manager to sell securities and thus often creates capital gains that will be taxed to the remaining shareholders in that fund. That was the problem with *market timing* years ago. Does that seem fair? Of course not! That's what we refer to as 'market impact.' I hasten to point out that the lack of that market impact is the hallmark of *passive investing*, which usually involves the use of asset class or standard index funds.

"The passive investing approach is highly tax-efficient because the passive investor remains invested in spite of market volatility. Why? Because they own the market globally, and their goal is to obtain returns commensurate with the *market returns*. The only time the passively managed mutual fund is revised occurs when the underlying asset class discontinues a particular stock and replaces it with another or when the entire portfolio is *rebalanced* in order to maintain the appropriate, and agreed upon, stock and bond mix as

# THE WALL STREET CASINO

> **Independent Advice**
> - Many Services/Independent Research
> - Due Diligence on Many Global Strategies
> - No "Marketing Fees"
> - Strategy "Upgrades" when Appropriate
> - Fee-Only Synergy with Client
> - Full Disclosure of All Fees
> - No Commissions
> - Unlimited Alternatives
> - Tax Deductibility of Fees
> - Low Market Impact

determined by the investor's need. The passive structure, of course, is far more cost efficient than the actively managed mutual fund because far less physical management occurs. The average internal expense ratio, therefore, is reduced from approximately 1.5% to as little as 0.17%. That savings accrues to the *bottom line* to benefit the investor!

"So, I appreciate and thank you for your kind attention and hope that you now have a better understanding of my concern about the inefficiencies of investment in America and the exporting of those inefficiencies to our country and to all other countries."

"Bravo!" bellowed Adam as he rose to shake the professor's hand. The professor assured all present that he would be pleased to attend the next excursion and excused himself. The trio, bidding farewell to Mr. Jacobs and Professor Maboto, set out to continue their journey from Cape Town to Hong Kong in the East.

# CHAPTER FIVE

Adam and Jane both agreed that the professor's comments were surely accurate, yet they both understood that capitalism and independence built America. After all, American investors were able to create the necessary funds and war material to win previous wars and to support the industrialization of America. They agreed further that the professor was right in his statement that the efficiency of our capital markets had declined remarkably. Regulators in America need to correct the Wall Street deficiencies as soon as possible. Adam pointed out that Rex Sinquefield, a leading advocate of "passive asset class index fund" investments declared, "If active money managers were racehorses…they would be glue." That line, he said, always gets a laugh!

Adam also offered a few brief wealth building success factors. He suggested that all investors should:

- Pay off all credit card debt
- Maintain a long-term investment plan
- Make systematic contributions with electronic transfer
- Save money religiously
- Diversify among asset classes—globally
- Rebalance their portfolio consistently
- Convert their *retail* mutual funds to more efficient asset-class index alternatives
- Remember not to confuse life insurance with investments

## THE WALL STREET CASINO

- Accept the tax burden and the advisor's fees as a byproduct of investing
- Seek out a qualified, <u>fee-only</u>, licensed investment advisor and stick with them
- Never use a debit card to access their 401(k)
- Be certain to take your "Required Minimum Distribution" on your qualified retirement account at age 70½ to avoid the 50% penalty

At last, Jane realized and admitted that her relationship with her broker had been misleading and that she wanted to learn a great deal more about the most efficient ways to invest today.

As they traveled south, then east around the Cape of Good Hope, Bryce and Mr. Smith discussed the kaleidoscope of the South African people and cultures. They discussed the great tropical rain forests, savannas teaming with wildlife, sun-scorched deserts, and sprawling modern cities. Mr. Smith pointed out that the great civilization of the ancient Egyptians was actually born from the fertile land of the Nile delta. He also alluded to the 700 million people who inhabit this great continent and to their ethnic and cultural diversity; more than eight hundred languages are spoken across the continent, and scores of ethnic groups can be identified. He pointed out that, by the end of the 1970s, all of Africa was free of their colonial shackles. This luxuriant capitalistic culture was now free to seek its own identity and destiny. Mr. Smith is convinced that it will continue to succeed.

# CHAPTER FIVE

# Notes

# ROBERT KNEISLEY

## Author's Comment

*There you have it. The Wall Street establishment had grown both staid...and inefficient.* The self-policing authority originally established as the National Association of Securities Dealers (now FINRA) had grown powerful enough to create their own electronic stock exchange. How could this happen? How could the charter be so loosely written? Where were the bureaucrats who control such things? Where were the regulators? Oh! They ARE the regulators. We must ask ourselves— *"Ízzat faire?"*

The pendulum always seems to swing too far left or right. The self-policing authority appears to be responsible for having created negotiated commissions, *which gave birth to commission* discounting *that resulted in a reduction in exorbitant Wall Street profits demanding a new profit center. And a new profit center sprung up! It is interesting to see how* free markets *function. Personally, I feel that investors would surely benefit if the Security and Exchange Commission required brokered, retail mutual funds, as well as all others, to report* <u>all their internal fees</u> *(including their clearing costs!).*

My wife Jo and I had the pleasure of attending a national symposium sponsored by the Profit Sharing Council of America a few years back. The audience was made up of leading 401(k) sponsors who oversaw the management of billions of dollars in 401(k) plans to benefit retirees. Among the speakers, there were a total of four attorneys who covered substantially different topics but all alluded to the importance of 401(k) providers understanding all the internal costs of their 401(k) portfolios in the event they were audited by the Department of Labor. They pointed out that substantial penalties could ensue.

*Not able to continue to withstand such heresy, I inquired of the fourth attorney as to whether he envisioned any time soon that the SEC would require that mutual funds report their clearing costs. Jaws dropped. People looked incredulously at each other in disbelief. I felt vindicated in my having asked the question but expected little progressive response. I was correct. The speaker artfully danced around the issue for several minutes and then exited stage left.*

### Trading Costs and Turnover Rates

*Professors Gregory Kadlec of Virginia Tech, Roger Edelen of Boston College, and Richard Evans of the University of Virginia authored a study completed in 2006 entitled "Scale Effects of Mutual Fund Performance." The study involved 1,706 domestic mutual funds from 1995 through 2006 and examined "bid/asked"\* spreads on all fund trades. The study determined that annual spread costs for small cap funds averaged 2.85%, mid-cap funds averaged 1.73%, and large cap funds averaged 0.77%. These figures, of course, must be added to the clearing costs (brokerage commissions paid on each trade), the fund's expense ratio, and any sales commissions paid by the investor. Professor Edelen confirmed in July 2008 that funds seldom report internal trading costs. Again, "Iźzat faire?"*

*It follows then, that internal fund turnover rates vary widely from fund to fund thus impacting the internal trading costs. Turnover rates for passively managed index funds are minimal, and the resulting market impact for fund investors is small. Note the tables below that quantify turnover for passively managed funds versus the radical outliers that feature an unbelievable amount of trading activity. "Iźzat faire?"*

*\*Bid: Price at which a market maker will buy a security. Ask: Price at which a seller is willing to sell a security. (The difference is profit.)*

# ROBERT KNEISLEY

## Passive vs. Hyperactive *Outliers*

The tables below illustrate the passive vs. active management extremes from 2001 through 2007.

**S&P 500 Passively Managed Equity Funds**

| Year | Macro Class | Avg. Portfolio Turnover (%) | Micro Obj. |
|------|-------------|------------------------------|------------|
| 2001 | EQ | 14.33 | SPSP |
| 2002 | EQ | 12.08 | SPSP |
| 2003 | EQ | 8.16 | SPSP |
| 2004 | EQ | 9.84 | SPSP |
| 2005 | EQ | 9.64 | SPSP |
| 2006 | EQ | 8.49 | SPSP |
| 2007 | EQ | 12.38 | SPSP |

**Excessive Avg. Portfolio Turnover Rates (Index Pure)**

| Year | Macro Class | Avg. Portfolio Turnover (%) | Micro Obj. | Fund Name |
|------|-------------|------------------------------|------------|-----------|
| 2001 | EQ | 5388 | MLGE | PROFUNDS:NASDAQ-100;INV |
| 2002 | EQ | 4550 | SCGE | PROFUNDS:SM-CAP GRO;SVC |
| 2002 | EQ | 3616 | MCGE | PROFUNDS:MID-CAP GRO;SVC |
| 2003 | EQ | 2235 | MCGE | PROFUNDS:MID-CAP GRO;INV |
| 2005 | EQ | 2018 | MLGE | RYDEX:LG-CAP GROWTH;H |
| 2005 | EQ | 2018 | MLGE | RYDEX:LG-CAP GROWTH;A |
| 2002 | EQ | 1850 | SCVE | PROFUNDS:SM-CAP VAL;SVC |
| 2003 | EQ | 1359 | LGVE | PROFUNDS:LG-CAP VAL;INV |
| 2004 | EQ | 1293 | MCGE | PROFUNDS:MID-CAP GRO;SVC |
| 2004 | EQ | 1288 | LCCE | PROFUNDS:LG-CAP GRO;SVC |
| 2005 | EQ | 1287 | LCCE | PROFUNDS:LG-CAP GRO;INV |
| 2007 | EQ | 1029 | MLGE | RYDEX:LG-CAP GROWTH;A |

Source: Lipper

Investors planning their retirement deserve better. Perhaps, there should exist a broad investor's coalition that could actually police the entire industry and coerce our bureaucrats to offer further protections to the investing public. I would hope that the Profit Sharing Council itself might take up the challenge. It seems however, that life is too short. Most attorneys dismiss such an argument with the statement that we live in an imperfect world. Attorneys can appreciate that posture...and profit from it.

Mr. David L. Wray, President of the Profit Sharing/401(k) Council of America, recently stated that 55 million Americans are now 401(k) participants with a current account value of $3 trillion. Therefore, the average value of participants' individual 401(k) plans would be $55,000. Will these future retirees "arrive in style?"

# CHAPTER FIVE

*Maybe not; target funds (designed to target varied retirement dates) are an extremely popular investment within 401(k)s. According to a recent Morningstar study of the twenty-five largest target date funds, some had between 20%–30% invested in either mortgage bonds or financial stocks—this, while we find ourselves in a mortgage meltdown with foreclosures soaring 120% in the second quarter, 2008. Morningstar stated that the average exposure of these funds to those sectors runs about 13%, which seems excessive.*

*Because of the above major missteps, 401(k) participants, and indeed all investors, require very broad asset allocation as the only safe harbor during the current bear market. For non-qualified account holders, taxes and inflation exacerbate the problem. Even reallocating a portion of one's portfolio to bonds (fixed income) could be destructive because the current inflationary trend could force the Federal Reserve to increase interest rates to combat inflation. Doing so would <u>deflate</u> bond prices. We find ourselves once again in the throes of financial crisis as a direct result of poor regulation and greed. "Ízzat faire?"*

# ROBERT KNEISLEY

# Chapter Six

The threesome was seated up on the bridge, as *Aquarius* got underway. The radiotelephone rang. Bryce grimaced as he realized the caller was Jane's broker, Mr. Marmot. He shuddered as he listened to Jane explain that she was an excursionist on this epic voyage. She even explained the New York leg of their journey and where they planned to berth *Aquarius*. (Bryce reasoned that the less Mr. Marmot knew of her whereabouts and activities the better.) Greedily, broker Marmot suggested that she could sell *put options*[7] on the descending stocks in the trust portfolio in an effort to capitalize on the downtrend. Yet another speculative strategy that he recommended depended totally on his being able to foresee the direction of the market going forward. Jane smiled demurely as she rejected both his strategic investment suggestion and his invitation to visit yet again. She bid him goodbye and placed her hand on Bryce's as they both smiled at each other knowingly. A decidedly warmer

---

7   A contract between a seller (writer) and the buyer permitting the buyer the right, but not the obligation, to sell a commodity or financial instrument to the seller of the contract at a time and price certain.

breeze now seemed to be wafting through the open curtains of the bridge. Human pheromones drifted throughout the area like fireflies in July.

"Well, Jane, it's on to Xiamggang and another, but more aggressive, capitalistic culture!" exclaimed Bryce as he maneuvered *Aquarius* north of the Cape of Good Hope.

"Xiamggang?" inquired Jane. "I thought we were destined to go to Hong Kong?"

"That's exactly right, Jane. Xiamggang is the same location…just an older name. We are destined for Hong Kong and should be there momentarily."

"Bryce, I know that China has become a huge producer of products sold worldwide today, but I'm afraid I don't understand much about China, let alone Asia in general. Can you tell me why we chose China or Hong Kong in particular?"

Bryce smiled knowingly and said, "My specialty is investment management, Jane. Perhaps you should go below and discuss the history in detail with Adam who I'm sure is more than capable of giving you a robust response to your question."

Jane smiled appreciatively as she exited through the aft door on the bridge and descended the stairs to the salon. She entered the salon to a boisterous welcome by Mr. Smith. "Aye, Lass! And how are you this fine afternoon?" he questioned in his thick Scottish brogue.

"Just great! Thank you. Bryce told me to come down and talk to you about our next visit, which I understand is Hong Kong."

# CHAPTER SIX

"It surely is! A visit to a small region that is part of China, which is part of Asia, where three out of five people on earth live! Jane, as you may know, Asia is by far the world's most heavily populated continent.

"The Great Wall of China is over 2,200 years old and is 4,300 miles in length. In early history, it served to protect the inner conclave from invasion, and it has been suspected that it also restrained the inhabitants within the walls from departure. Interestingly, Jane, Japan went through a similar period of isolation, which was termed 'Sakoko.' It started in 1635 and lasted for 200 years. Commodore Matthew Perry steamed into the Bay of Edo on July 8, 1853 and displayed to *old Tokyo* the awesome power of his five ships' cannons. He then politely requested that Japan open trade with the West. Thanks to the brash commodore, there exists prosperity in that region today and for the past half century. Again, Jane, free markets work!

"Labor unions, of course, have been around as long as laborers. The historic relationship between labor and management, however, usually finds the pendulum swinging to extremes. Such may well have been the case from 1940 through the turn of the century when labor unions blossomed globally. Who could have dreamed that the great power of labor in America would compete with the great rivers of global competition resulting in NAFTA and the transfer of America's manufacturing base? The trend will surely cripple unions' progress and may even reach to the heavily unionized government sector, which could result in tax savings to all Americans. So goes the ebb and flow.

## THE WALL STREET CASINO

"The existence of unions has been compared to the movie entitled *Willy Wonka and the Chocolate Factory*. The movie depicts a very successful corporation (Wonka Chocolates) and employees that betrayed Mr. Wonka by stealing his secret recipes. Mr. Wonka abruptly closes the chocolate factory and fires all employees. Much like the world today, he automates the factory with modern robotics and pleases the children when the factory reopens.

"Asia could be the next growing stronghold for unionism. Asia represents a microcosm of the entire globe! The population is roughly 3.8 billion souls and recent economic and technological development has allowed China, Indonesia, Korea, Singapore, and Japan to rise to great international prominence. I think the twenty-first century will be dubbed the 'Asian Century' in history. I also feel that you will thoroughly enjoy your visit to capitalistic Hong Kong because it is an anomaly that demonstrates the huge success of its now capitalistic approach while still being under the auspices of communist China. It is a true laboratory study. Hong Kong has surely proven to the Asian community that *free markets* do work effectively. Jane, we just passed capitalistic South Korea, which glistens at night with electric lighting that can be easily viewed from satellites. There is no such light in Communist North Korea."

"Free markets underscore the difference, Jane," Adam explained that Chinese is the most spoken language in the world and that China has only one time zone.

Mr. Smith pointed out that the long history of Hong

# CHAPTER SIX

Kong dates back to imperial China, an era that occurred from 221 B.C. through the 1800s. He explained that the Japanese occupied Hong Kong in the 1940s and that modern Hong Kong came under British rule in the 1950s. In the 1960s, Hong Kong further developed its textile industry as the foundation of its early economy and went on to boost industry in support of its cultural revolution, which placed Hong Kong on a new political stage. Hong Kong had witnessed dramatic growth because of capitalism throughout the last four decades of the twentieth century.

Mr. Smith went on to explain that in 1982, the British Prime Minister Margaret Thatcher endorsed the continuation of British rule, which led to Hong Kong being recognized as one of the wealthiest areas in the Far East. The economic reform led to an agreed upon 1997 territorial *handover*, which did, in fact, take place on July 1, 1997 when Hong Kong was handed over to the People's Republic of China by the United Kingdom. Mr. Smith indicated that there was never any doubt in his mind that capitalism would be enshrined in this glittering apex of success.

Adam went on to explain that in 1990, the Shanghai Stock Exchange came into existence. He lamented that the exchange did not represent a truly *free market*. Rather, there were separate categories of shares—those that could be held by the public and those that could be held only by the state or "legal persons."[8] Adam speculated that mainland China still held strong ties to the growth of the economy

---

8   Burton Malkiel, *Journal of Indexes* (January/February 2008):10–14.

and to the control of outside ownership through troublesome governance implications and the market impact on majority-state-owned banks. "Free markets demonstrate their ability to overrule controlled markets with obvious success," he asserted. He further explained that mainland China succumbed to the Communist Party of China rule in the Chinese Civil War in the 1950s. The Republic of China was effectively banished to Taiwan in the 1950s. Having arrived at the port of Hong Kong, Mr. Smith suggested that Jane prepare to disembark.

It was only moments until their vessel was docked at Hong Kong among hundreds of unusual looking vessels. Most vessels sported a great crane on deck. It appeared that material could be transferred in Victoria Harbor, rather than at the dock within the grasp of customs officials. Jane could not help but wonder how much contraband moved in this unique fashion. It seemed a land of intrigue.

As they strolled toward the Quarterdeck Club in Wanchai, Mr. Smith recounted the trillion dollar global trading practice that this socialist country actively pursues. "Within the next ten years, this entire economy and culture will be revised dramatically," extolled Mr. Smith. He further illustrated his point by refer-

Hong Kong Port

# CHAPTER SIX

ring to the fact that as a small child he noted that business relationships created friendship. His father's best friends were business acquaintances—the very people that actually benefited the business his father was in. Both Bryce and Jane agreed that such a relationship existed even to the extent that we now have service clubs such as Rotary and Kiwanis that are designed to encourage such relationships. Adam Smith pointed out that this is probably the ultimate answer to world peace.

The problem is that there exists a very wide wage disparity between third world socialist countries and the developed nations. Mr. Smith contended that the gap would close quickly. At 11:00 a.m., they arrived at a Hong Kong marketplace. Dried duck was hanging from strings at small booths along the roadside. They noted the popularity of Chinese chess. Scores of natives, young and old, enjoyed playing the simple game as they visited with one another. There were hundreds of very small counter areas and numerous booths displaying jewelry, vegetables, and products from both China and the free world.

Adam Smith approached one of the *shopkeepers* and inquired regarding the shopkeeper's retirement plans. The Chinese entrepreneur pointed out that his dependency was entirely upon his government for benefits. Convinced of the temporary nature of the socialist culture, Mr. Smith inquired as to the entrepreneur's impression of the future permanence of the socialist approach. With some embarrassment, the shopkeeper admitted to the uncertainty that

## THE WALL STREET CASINO

surrounds the economic realities of socialism. Privately, Adam Smith was delighted. He believed, as most people well know, in free markets. The facts of the interview were not lost on Jane.

They stayed the night at the luxuriant Renaissance Harbour Hotel in the city and enjoyed a delightful breakfast after visiting with many more natives of China who echoed the same concerns the shopkeeper had indicated. They cruised Victoria Harbour that afternoon, noting the "water people" in numerous floating communities and visited the famous Jumbo floating restaurant.

*Renaissance Harbor Hotel*

Having some free time at last, Bryce seized the opportunity to invite Jane out for the evening. She accepted because she wanted to spend some qual-

*Jumbo Restaurant*

ity time with Bryce, and she surely needed this opportunity to vent her emotional distress to an expert who might be able to ease her concerns. Jane was humming Mancini's "Moon River." Bryce met Jane at her room and they walked

## CHAPTER SIX

together to the lounge and relaxed on the balcony overlooking lovely Victoria Harbour. Bryce indicated his satisfaction with Jane's acceptance of the modern investment concepts that he and Adam so deeply believed in. Jane confided that she felt close to despondency concerning her investment failure and her frustration with her stockbroker, Mr. Caesar Marmot.

Victoria Harbour

"Jane, I think I understand your situation, and I can tell you that you're not unique in your concerns. Most investors don't understand that there is a whole psychological field of study concentrating on what is professionally known today as 'Investor Behavioral Finance.' Behavioral finance has determined that we investors don't always behave rationally because we frequently react to imperfect, totally inaccurate, or incomplete information. I'd like to discuss your psychology as an individual investor, Jane. Would that be alright with you?"

"I suppose so, Bryce. But, I'm not sure that understanding how investors behave will change what's happening with our family's trust account and my impression of what's happening with the markets today. What am I missing?" Jane responded.

"You're absolutely right, Jane. The relationship is not obvious. However, by better understanding investor behavior, and your own behavior, you can make better investing decisions that are tailored to your specific needs and those of your family. Additionally, you can stay the course to reach your long-term investment goals, which many investors are unable to do. These two factors will improve your investment experience and certainly make you more comfortable. Besides, if I were a selfish guy, I would submit that this understanding could build a stronger relationship between you as the investor and me as your financial advisor. Dear heart, the more time I spend with you, the more convinced I become that I want to be somewhat more than your financial advisor. But, that's a whole different topic." Jane's blush was concealed by darkness.

"Right now, Jane, my perception of the root cause of your stress is what behavioral psychologists would call 'loss aversion.' Do you follow the stock market on a daily basis, and do you feel frustrated with short-term market movements?" Bryce inquired.

Jane exhibited a knowing smile as she nodded in the affirmative. "You're absolutely on target, Bryce. I obsess over short-term market movements...and Caesar now calls me daily, which only supports that obsession. I was brought up in a conservative family that taught me to pay attention to details. Is watching the stock market activity not appropriate?"

"Sure it is, Jane," Bryce responded. "But, having said that, I have to explain that if one is investing with a <u>long-</u>

# CHAPTER SIX

term perspective, one should avoid watching the daily fluctuations." Bryce quoted an Ibbotson Associates study that illustrated a basic series of compound annual returns of large company stocks and intermediate government bonds for one- through twenty-year periods, 1925 through 2000.

The study indicated that $1.00 invested in intermediate government bonds grew to $49.00 in the year 2000 while $1.00 invested in large company stocks grew to $2,587.00. Their study also reflected *volatility* (standard deviation)—reductions from 20.2% the first year, 8.5% in the fifth year, 5.6% in the tenth year, and only 3.6% in the twentieth year.

The study also determined that periods of investor *loss* diminished as the holding period lengthened—twenty-one periods of loss if held one year, seven periods if held five years, two periods if held ten years, and no periods of loss, on a rolling average, if held twenty years.

"You will note that the periods of loss diminish dramatically over time. It is important to remember that no one can guarantee the future, and surely past performance should never be perceived as a guarantee of the future. But, Jane, it is important to understand that for large company stocks in the twentieth year, there were no periods of loss for those who held stocks that long other than, perhaps, the effect of inflation (which impacts all investors). For intermediate government bonds, there would be no loss after as short a period of time as five years. In conclusion, if you could be pleased with your long-term investments over a longer term, you would eliminate your level of stress. But let's move on. Do you have a tendency to retain your losing investments and sell the winners, Jane?"

"I rely on my broker to make that investment decision," Jane responded. "Caesar does tend to sell winners and explains to me that there is not only little advantage to selling losers but also recommends *averaging down* on those positions that are losing money."

"The behaviorists call that reaction the 'disposition effect,' and it should be avoided because it can have a negative impact on your portfolio. The next problem that I think you share with millions of investors, Jane, centers around the fact that you measure your investment success in a secular fashion, relating only to your portfolio's performance rather than looking at the overall net worth of yourself or your family. Am I correct?"

"That's my current overriding concern, Bryce. And, I would have to say you are correct," Jane responded.

"That's a very common fault. It amounts to looking at the little picture versus the big picture, and the psychologists call that 'narrow framing.' That psychological phenomenon is right up there with what they call 'mental accounting.' That term attempts to explain the fact that investors place less value on the wealth they have grown as opposed to their original principal when making investment decisions. It's a concept not unlike the *house money* phenomenon with gamblers in casinos. Mental accounting is also a psychological weakness that we must all guard against. I should

# CHAPTER SIX

also relate a bit of gray humor, Jane, when I reflect on the perception that investors have when they succeed versus when investments go south. Such *hindsight bias* is amusing in that investors tend to perceive, as we all do, that success was their decision; however, the lack of success can easily be laid at the altar of the advisor. Such regret arises because a client perceives a bad outcome from a decision made in the past. Most of us are reluctant to own up to such an error."

## Notes

## CHAPTER SIX

# Author's Comment

*Jo and I had the great pleasure of visiting Hong Kong a few years ago. We found it to be a very cosmopolitan city that was modern in every fashion. The natives of Hong Kong appeared to be very similar to Americans, from their industrial activities through their social styles and even their fluent English language.*

*We were both ill prepared, however, for the authentic Chinese cuisine. Fortunately, we found a lovely hotel two blocks away that served steamship round of beef. It was delightful. We noticed that the grain of the roast ran in many directions, indicating that it was, perhaps, water buffalo rather than the customary American beef. Nonetheless, we enjoyed that meal, the culture, the obvious Chinese free market entrepreneurship, and the free Chinese people of Hong Kong.*

### The Core of Investor's Satisfaction is... EXPECTATIONS!

As mentioned earlier, retail brokers are trained to sell securities or products that have recently been successful. Doing so satisfies human nature but breeds dissatisfaction as soon as past performance lags. That is why so many investors fail to remain invested long-term... and long-term is the "sweet spot" for prudent retirement wealth building.

If the sales person illustrates a variable investment return averaging 15% over five years, the investor is naturally disillusioned and disappointed with anything less. The original number seems indelibly imprinted on the substrate of their subconscious.

The wiser, fee-only advisor realizes the psychological relationship, and rather than simply "selling a track record" that likely will not repeat with consistency, he/she uses past history to educate clients regarding market cycles. Doing so represents a priceless service to the client because he/she is then able to manage his/her own <u>expectations</u> when markets decline. Worth repeating, investment success requires time, and bear markets, while they repeat, support the sawtooth ascending pattern that is typical of a sound wealth-building program.

Another weird anomaly seems to exist when an advisor states that bear markets last fourteen months, and bull markets last seventy. Some investors reason that when substantial capital gains are created, they should be captured, so they are not consumed by the next inevitable bear market cycle.

Capturing such short-term profits is not simply unnecessary. It is downright damaging to the compounding cycle, creates tax losses or taxable gains, robs the investment manager of the opportunity to reallocate to securities that history has shown can literally explode when the early bull market cycle occurs, and lastly, usually results in the investor frittering away the funds that were withdrawn. Furthermore, while fear drives the emotional response to sell, greed is hard pressed to ring the investor's bell to signal an optimal time to get back <u>into</u> the market.

My advice, and the prudent path recommended by the wiser <u>fee-based</u> advisor, is to stay globally allocated in a balanced account for the long haul and rebalance as needed to maintain your mutually agreed upon mix of stocks, bonds, and cash. Doing so not only reduces the anxiety that leads to lower back pain but also enhances restful sleep thus... extending your retirement years. In reality then, a bear market is a truncated opportunity! Stay the course.

# Chapter Seven

"Do you watch much television, Jane?" Bryce inquired.

"Not a great deal," she responded. "But I certainly do try to keep up with current events and watch an occasional movie. Why do you ask?"

"I bring that up because the retail brokerage community and insurance industries spend billions of dollars in advertising annually. Such advertising encourages investors to watch the markets about as closely as we watch national and international sporting events. They are preying on our fear and greed. That's a dead wrong scenario for long-term investors."

"It would certainly seem so," Jane agreed.

Bryce smiled and continued. "The behavioral psychologists tell

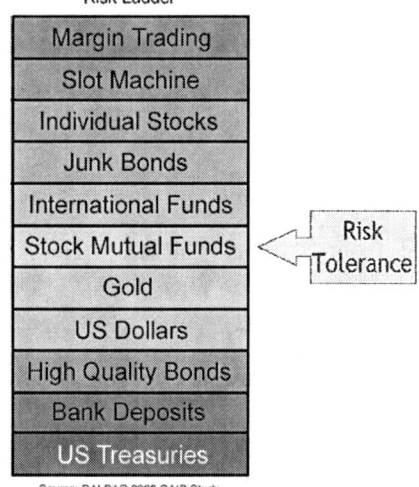

Risk Ladder

| Margin Trading |
| Slot Machine |
| Individual Stocks |
| Junk Bonds |
| International Funds |
| Stock Mutual Funds |
| Gold |
| US Dollars |
| High Quality Bonds |
| Bank Deposits |
| US Treasuries |

← Risk Tolerance

Source: DALBAR 2008 QAIB Study

us that we suffer from a 'media response' syndrome that causes us to feel the psychological impulse to *do something* when we perceive that we have received new information, either positive or negative.

"Remember, short-term activity, whether political, business, social, or economic has very little bearing on long-term investment performance. In fact, mere response is related directly to a term the psychologists call 'herding'. As the name suggests, Jane, herding is the tendency of investors to join other investors with a *herd mentality* and most often it results in an investment *bubble* that eventually bursts and hurts many investors. Such activity is only possible if there is an excessive amount of optimism and overconfidence, which is the next behavioral problem to which the psychologists allude. We always think that good things will happen to us and that bad things will happen to others. Such overconfidence can lead to rank speculation, and should also be avoided.

"To reduce speculation the academics have learned to globally diversify their *asset class* index funds with negative correlation. Doing so results in a *passive* strategy that many have dubbed the strategy 'for all stock market seasons.'

"Do you feel that your portfolio is properly allocated at this time, Jane?"

"In all honesty, Bryce, I am not sure if I even understand what proper allocation entails," Jane volunteered. Bryce briefly explained the relationship between conserva-

## CHAPTER SEVEN

tive investments and rank speculation. (Note the previous "Risk Ladder" and the fact that margin trading is directly above speculation on slot machines.)

"I appreciate your candor, Jane. Back in 1953, Harry Markowitz was a student at the University of Chicago. He created the concept of broad diversification and asset allocation as a means of reducing investment volatility (the up and down gyrations), which we perceive as risk. The approach is now known as Modern Portfolio Theory. That theory led to the Capital Asset Pricing Model developed by Professor William F. Sharpe at Stanford University. I think it's safe to say, Jane, that most investors don't understand the importance of global diversification, proper asset allocation, and the necessary application of *negative coefficients* within a properly diversified portfolio. That is to say that there must be a means for investors to access such institutional quality portfolio control. *Fee-only* investment advisors are the proper experts that can implement these programs most effectively.

"Doing so is absolutely critical to your success because such *passive* asset-class index fund investments, i.e., baskets of securities representing the fifteen asset classes, have a number of benefits for you. They can substantially reduce the internal cost of investing relative to retail mutual funds, decrease capital gains taxes, and increase the tax deductibility of the expenses of investing. The result is not only that these savings fall to the investor's bottom line, but they also result in reduced volatility and the potential for increased returns over time. Jane, has this brief discussion regarding investor behavior put your mind any more at ease?"

"Bryce, I thank you. Yes, I would say that I am more comfortable now than I have been in many weeks. Thank you for your concern." Jane leaned to the side and placed a gentle kiss on Bryce's cheek. He rested his hand on Jane's, and they watched the sun collapse into the beautiful horizon over Victoria Harbour.

Waking early, the trio had a light breakfast and, observing wonderful cruising weather, they traveled to their vessel. Mr. Smith suggested that Vladivostok, Russia, would be their next destination, offering surprising contrasts in their exciting journey. He extolled the virtues of capitalism over socialism and explained how the perception of how what we know as "greed" can benefit all. It took only minutes to ready the vessel to travel the short distance northeast. The South Atlantic was now in the west and the Yellow Sea was to the east. Adventure was surely ahead as they traveled at what seemed light speed.

Once more retiring to the salon of *Aquarius*, Mr. Smith relaxed on the sofa, his right arm resting atop the sofa back and his left hand embracing his scotch. Jane sat pensively anticipating her next educational session. Mr. Smith's Scottish

Aquarius' Pilot House

## CHAPTER SEVEN

accent seemed to thicken as he said, "As I observe these various cultures, I am reminded of the foundations of our existence. For me, being from Scotland, the game of golf was prominent in all our casual levity. I recall one July afternoon when we had organized a foursome, one of the less mentally capable of our members suggested that it would be fun to wake up on Christmas morning and go directly to the golf course for a round of golf without an argument from our wives. To my amazement, two of my colleagues thought that would be a splendid idea. I, weakened by my gentlemanly ways, was forced to agree. When that cold morning dawned, we all met at the golf course. The first golf colleague said, 'Aye, this golf game has cost me substantial gold! I was forced to purchase my wife a gold necklace to save our marriage.'

"The second colleague stated, 'So too have I parted with much gold. My wife is home going through travel catalogs because I promised her a fully paid two-week vacation!' At that moment, all eyes turned to me. Completely intimidated by the novelty of this catharsis, I explained that I expended a great deal of wealth on a new carriage for my wife in order to preserve our marriage and attend this unusual golf outing. We all stared at the dullard who suggested this social contrivance and he stated, 'I deeply regret that you gentlemen have gone through such expense for this golf game. For my part, upon awakening, I caressed my dear wife and wished her a Merry Christmas. It is, I said, a great morning for Christmas intimacy or perhaps a game of golf. And, she said, 'You'll need a sweater.'"

## THE WALL STREET CASINO

It seemed a bonding moment for Mr. Smith and Jane as they both enjoyed the whimsical story and laughed heartily. Mr. Smith seemed to relax even more. "Russia, as you may know, possesses more than adequate supplies of many of the world's most valued natural resources, particularly those required to support a modern economy. She is blessed with a well-educated labor force and possesses substantial technical prowess. But Russia suffers from poor infrastructure and inefficient supply systems that disable the possibility of efficient utilization of her resources.

"Ecological abuse has resulted in some areas, such as in Pokrovsky Park, becoming polluted to such an extent that they represent an ecological disaster zone. At present, only a few areas of Vladivostok have permissible levels of contamination. Why? Vladivostok is home to some eighty industrial sites that are environmentally unfriendly. These include their shipbuilding complexes, power stations, printing, fur farming, and mining facilities. Much like our California, the topography is low in the densely populated areas, and winds are ineffective in clearing the atmosphere of contamination. The environment might be the key cause of the modest decrease in population Vladivostok is witnessing. It is, however, still a fair sized city of about 550,000 souls."

The intercom crackled with Bryce's announcement that a radiotelephone call had been awaiting Jane's response. It was broker Caesar Marmot! He was calling again to learn more of Jane's travels and future destinations. Jane was

## CHAPTER SEVEN

very forthcoming and explained that, according to Mr. Smith, they would be visiting a local finance professor in Vladivostok. Mr. Marmot seemed intimidated. He correctly surmised that Mr. Smith and Bryce harbored a conflicting investment philosophy that challenged his intellectual premises. The information Jane provided to Mr. Marmot only increased his already nervous concerns.

As he nervously twisted his mole hair, he reminded Jane again of his admiration and affection for her and tried desperately to explain his weak investment philosophy. In her defense, Jane volunteered that she understood from Mr. Smith that they would be visiting with Professor Ivan Storchak, the Dean of Finance at the local university in Vladivostok. Caesar Marmot was feeling quite defeated when he asked what their next destination was. Overhearing the entire conversation, Mr. Smith was concerned when Jane responded that they were headed for New York and Wall Street.

"Great! I'll meet you there!" Marmot hastily announced as he briskly hung up the telephone. Jane now seemed to realize the conflicted position in which she had placed Bryce, Adam, and herself.

The intercom once again interrupted as Bryce explained that they were coming into the Vladivostok Harbor and that they would be staying at the newly constructed Hyundai Hotel overlooking the harbor. Peering out a starboard side window, Jane noticed that the harbor was beautifully ablaze with an early morning sun that highlighted a velvet soft mist over the urban area. Looking at her wristwatch, she surmised that it was only the second day of their journey. Mr. Smith's time compression was truly amazing! At that ungainly moment, Mr. Smith began to chuckle. Not a normal chuckle but rather, a deep and growing chortle that seemed to grow the more his thought processes expanded. "What's so funny?" Jane inquired.

Vladivostok Harbor

Now laughing, Mr. Smith stated that he could recall that on his last trip to Russia, he met a Russian who was applying for a driver's license at the local constabulary. He said he watched the man take his eye examination and the optician showed him a card with the letters CZWIX-NOSTACZ. The optician asked if he could read it, and to her amusement, the man responded, "Read it? I know the guy!" They both enjoyed another hardy laugh before Mr. Smith got quasi-serious and began to explain the Russian culture to Jane.

"For over half a century, the Russian economy along with the rest of the Soviet Union operated on the basis of central planning. Unlike Hong Kong, and somewhat like South Africa, the government controlled virtually all means of production, investment, and consumption for its populace throughout its entire economy. Jane, the Communist Party made all the decisions. Such central planning

## CHAPTER SEVEN

represents a system that left Russia with a legacy that will surely hinder its transition to a market economy. And, Jane we all know, free markets work! The Berlin Wall was torn down during the Reagan administration, but changing the Russian culture, like the Russian economy, is a bit like pushing on a chain. Russia, however, has undergone strategic economic reform since the 1990s.

"As a matter of fact, in October of 1991, a scant two months before the official collapse of the Soviet regime, Boris Yeltsin and his advisors established a program of radical reform. The 1990s represented a turbulent period of massive economic change and stultifying inflation. In 1993, the annual rate of inflation declined from 2,520% to a startlingly modest rate of 240%! Jane, can you imagine trying to invest to build personal wealth when inflation is 2500%? For that matter, 240% annually would be an impossible challenge, would it not?"

"Does that mean, Adam, that investors would have to earn the same rate as inflation just to preserve the wealth they already have?"

"You've struck the peg squarely, my dear!" Mr. Smith said with a broad smile. "Remember, the two great enemies of all investors are inflation and taxation. The total return, that is, dividends, interest, and capital gain, on our investments must go well beyond the rate of inflation plus the rate of taxation on the dividends, interest, or gains in order to make true progress. That is not a simple proposition.

"Extending that thought, the greatest enemies we have today in addition to those two demons are represented by credit card borrowing, malicious banking and mortgage practices, and the existence of what I call 'quick cash sites.' They all charge onerous penalties or interest rates. History has proven that humans are easily trained to accept and utilize these services and processes that, over the longer term, are detrimental to their financial health. This has been proven with gambling, the lottery, and more recently, the adjustable rate mortgage, which transfers much of the risk from the banking institution to the consumer.

"It is unfortunate to note that the latest trend involves mortgages being sold from the originating banking institution to other banks and non-bank entities and thence to the Wall Street brokerages. Wall Street then repackages these mortgages in various unit dimensions that are designed to appeal to the many different types of investors that desire *fixed income* investments. Wall Street earns money regardless of the direction of the stock market. Remember also that they make a great deal of money because of internal expenses with these types of products. Solid evidence of the excessive profits garnered by the brokerage industry is apparent in the chief executive officers' huge salaries and the out-sized multi-million dollar bonuses to *gifted* analysts and other key employees during the holidays. Such bonuses total billions of dollars! These practices, Jane, will lead to no good. Regulators should control these trends; however, citizens can never truly depend upon the bureaucracy to forestall major financial calamity.

"It has been said that politicians are much like diapers, Jane. They must be changed often and for the same reasons.

# CHAPTER SEVEN

That is yet another reason why we, as individual investors, must make every effort to build our personal wealth most efficiently to overcome those periods of calamity. Be aware that one such common calamity is called 'retirement.'"

Jane looked deeply into Mr. Smith's tired eyes as she sipped her iced tea, and he poured yet another scotch.

## Notes

# CHAPTER SEVEN

# Author's Comment

*Perhaps POGO was right! If our own emotions are the enemy, "the enemy is us"! It follows that if we are so emotionally driven, perhaps the fewer micro decisions that we make regarding our investments, the better. There is no question that on the fringes of market activity, it is possible from time to time to find individual stocks that can be profitably owned. But such trading on a short-term basis is most often unsuccessful. If an investor can hold a security for decades, the level of success is very much improved.*

*The success of the more efficient passive investing lies in the fact that the process reduces taxes and trading costs, saves the investor mountains of time, and averages out the volatility factor globally so that investors can maintain their long-term objective. My father stated that one should not worry about the compounding of interest but rather concentrate on placing more funds into the portfolio. He had many such beliefs that were the foundation of his enduring success.*

### Beyond Emotions... America Stands at a Crossroads in 2008

*I never recommended a bank stock because their accounting procedures seemed conflicted. Banks boost profits by increasing the liability side of their balance sheet! At the risk of sounding old-fashioned, isn't that about the same as buying securities on "margin?" It certainly is.*

*When you couple that with a Federal Reserve that is inattentive to such speculation, might that be why we find ourselves in 2008 at what many believe to be our "economic delta?"*

*When the real estate bubble burst, the bankers lost billions of dollars. Experts estimate that the banking "leverage fever" might result in as*

## ROBERT KNEISLEY

*much as $1 trillion in credit contraction globally. ("Ízzat faire?") Because credit is the lubricant of world commerce, our global recovery could be much slower than previously anticipated.*

# Chapter Eight

Having docked *Aquarius* at the Vladivostok harbor, Captain Bryce and Mr. Smith secured the vessel, installed the shore power cable, and attached the water system. Bryce explained that he had arranged all the passport details, and they spent almost no time at all processing paperwork. They were scheduled to meet Professor Storchok for lunch at the hotel.

Arriving there a bit early for lunch, Jane was impressed with the modern style that was obviously of Korean origin. After registering, they arrived at the restaurant and observed the finance professor seated with a perfect view of the harbor. Professor Storchok was of a stocky build with a warm smile and a firm handshake. He greeted Bryce and Adam joyously with a double handshake, a pat on the back, and a generous hug

Hyundai Hotel

for both. Jane was impressed with his outgoing warmth as he embraced her right hand with both his hands and then brought her hand to his cheek for a traditional 'face hug,' accepting her instantly as a friend.

They ordered tea and Jane sat back absorbing the conversation, which tended toward the many past business relationships the three had shared. The professor exchanged pleasantries with Jane, and they ordered their entrees. Mr. Smith soon guided the conversation toward the recent economic history of Russia and invited the professor to bring Jane up-to-date.

The professor began to explain the Stalin Era, speaking slowly with obvious enunciation effort due to his heavy Russian accent. "It has been difficult, Jane. As recently as 1997, our economy was still influenced by Joseph Stalin's concepts. We have suffered through many 'five-year plans' and adjusted many programs seeking to control our economy because our primary belief was that we could benefit the greater number by controlling man's natural tendency toward greed." The professor cast a knowing glance and quick smile at Adam. "Our State Planning Committee established targets for different planning periods, and regional planning committees would then refine and implement those targets.

"Unfortunately, we have not developed the technology to measure our progress. Everything flowed from the top down, not much from the bottom up. We have had some seventy government ministries and state committees responsible for controlling their respective geographical ar-

# CHAPTER EIGHT

eas. Our system proved itself during the Nazi invasion because we could marshal great assets very quickly. America surely was more efficient in that process at wartime due to her efficient capital markets. The process also helped us become a superpower after the Second World War. In the 1980s, we had experienced very mixed results. Perestroika, our restructuring process, was proven ineffective when Gorbachev was in office. Only since 1991 when Boris Yeltsin took charge did we begin to develop a market economy through freer market-determined pricing. We have become a dim reflection of your economic system. Again, we lacked infrastructure. In 1992, we had massive inflation measuring more than 2500%!

"That's when we started deregulating prices under government control, which ignited price increases in the magnitude of over 200% in a single month! Inflation is still not totally under control but much lower now. Another step we have taken as a reflection of your own economy has been the privatization of many government industries and the issuance of shares of stock to 144 million citizens in Russia." The professor chuckled as he slammed his hands on the table and said, "Only one big difference! The holders of this stock could not sell them! They could only invest them in a thing called a 'voucher fund.' Many invested in the voucher funds at a fraction of the value of their shares, and the result was that there was a great concentration of ownership in only a few hands. We now have a better system and are able to invest in shares that can be sold on secondary markets.

## THE WALL STREET CASINO

"While Mr. Yeltsin accomplished a great deal through his privatization, our prominent Sovietologist, Marshall Goldman, has argued that Mr. Yeltsin's program should have included property ownership of land, should have reformed our currency, liberalized pricing structures, helped form new private companies, eliminated taxes on wages, focused more on fiscal policy control, and implemented the convertibility of the ruble. All this he desired <u>before</u> privatization! Could be so," the professor shrugged. Bryce and Adam nodded in agreement.

"So there was some downside effect?" Bryce inquired.

"Habsolutely!" responded the professor as he raised both hands above his head. "It was a disaster. The *insider privatization* caused billions of dollars in capital flight out of our Russian Central Banking System, and since the government was unwilling to increase salaries for educators to match the inflation rate, or even make salary payments on a timely basis, educators and scientists fled to the West."

The professor went on with more explanation: "The Asian Financial Crisis of 1998 caused a Russian Financial Crisis due to the reduced earnings from our oil exports. Then, the ruble fell in value, which resulted in a lack of payment on 40 billion dollars in ruble bonds. Inflation popped to 86% in 1999, and here we are today, surrounded by world trade, most of which we do not participate in. Remarkable!"

They all enjoyed a casual meal. The conversation found them asking and answering questions regarding Russia's

# CHAPTER EIGHT

monetary policy, government, labor, spending, taxation, the practice of law in Russia, the country's natural resources, and prominent industries. The professor answered each question eloquently. The direct result of attempted corrective measures was usually mixed performance due to the previously controlled economy. The professor stated that Russia needed stronger representation of its labor force. There was a great need for more equality among laborers and a more balanced labor/management relationship—thus, a freer market.

Adam interjected that he had been watching labor organizations all his adult life and beyond. He stressed that labor organizations are as old as industrialization and agricultural economic pursuits. He acknowledged that in the early 1900s, as before, child labor and long work hours in America were unjust.

"There is no question that organized labor has served an important purpose and continues to do so. However, when labor protection gains too much political power, the result is higher taxes on businesses and families, bloated bureaucracies that increasingly interfere with industry, and excessive control of schools by union chiefs rather than classroom teachers, taxpayers, and parents. So, Jane, there is even a limit to how valuable organized labor should be. I should point out that this is information that few politicians at any level wish to discuss. The price we pay in decreased productivity and progress can be enormous! The market in American manufacturing has become out-priced in our global economy. This is yet another testimony to the fact that overly controlled markets fail while free markets work. It is also strong testimony supporting our need to invest globally."

Adam Smith was happy to report that Russia was on the right track. He stated that trade in Russia would increase dramatically going forward if Russia continued its economic discipline with freer markets. That trade, he said, would be reciprocal and the Russian economy would grow at a much more rapid pace due to future foreign investment in Russian projects. Bryce explained that such economic reciprocity would also benefit investors worldwide through more foreign investment opportunity. The three bid a fond farewell to the professor after thanking him for his comments.

Jane was now armed with enough current information to be dangerous to Caesar Marmot. The thought of going to the very citadel of world trade and the center of commerce on Wall Street caused excitement she could hardly contain. "Bryce, it is true that our next stop is actually Wall Street?" asked Jane as they strolled toward the harbor.

"Next stop on our whirlwind tour! Everything is in place to dock there very shortly. I'm afraid that the timing of our visits may be causing considerable consternation with the customs officials, but they haven't actually stopped us yet. Assuming we get past customs in New York, we will be visiting with Dr. William Shrill, the noted expert regarding institutional, or *wholesale,* investment of a passive nature.

## CHAPTER EIGHT

"You had mentioned that your broker friend and relative, Mr. Marmot, plans to meet you in New York. Perhaps he would care to join our discussion and extend his intellectual knowledge regarding Modern Portfolio Theory and the more modern, efficient investment strategy we know as 'asset class index fund' investing?"

"Frankly, Bryce, I don't care if he never makes the connection. However, if he's willing to participate in that type of discussion he is more than welcome to attend as far as I am concerned," Jane responded.

Arriving at their motor yacht, they made ready all systems and departed through the Strait of La Perouse and the Bering Sea passage, headed for New York City. As the great distance vanished past the salon windows Mr. Smith gently chided Jane about the amount of luggage she brought with her that would have to be returned without ever having left the carrier due to the abbreviated nature of their voyage. "If only it could always be so," Jane said with a smile as she took her usual seat across from the sofa.

"So, my pretty Jane, the next leg of our journey will discern for you what works and why it works. I can assure you that 60% of retail money managers will underperform the overall stock market indexes in the long-term, and together, we will prove it. They do so for any number of reasons, not the least of which is the inherent cost to manage money. But just for fun, let's review a little history and see if your answer would be about the same as an analyst's or a money manager's in the retail marketing sector."

"You are aware, I'm sure, Jane, that technology in the form of the cell phone was created in about 1981 by Motorola. At the same time, there was a meat product that carried the unusual slogan 'crazy tasty.' The product was, of course, Spam, and the company was Hormel Foods. Given just those simple facts, which investment, Motorola or Hormel, would make the most sense to you if you were investing your money for growth back in 1981?"

"That's an easy one! It would certainly be Motorola because cell phones are pretty much everywhere we look," responded Jane.

"Aha!" proclaimed Mr. Smith as he bolted from the sofa and began to pace the floor. "You would have missed a great opportunity, Jane! The truth is, over the next 25 years, the total return for Motorola was a challenging 1568%. The return however, for Hormel foods was a staggering 5946%!

You obviously made a decision based upon your observation concerning the great number of cell phones versus the few encounters you had with the product known as Spam. One can assume that your answer was 90% an *emotional* response. Please be aware that the emotional response you exhibited is also the type of response an ana-

**Which would you choose in 1981**
Cell phones or canned pork shoulder?

**SPAM**
*is Crazy Tasty!*

**% Total return: 25 years ending December 2005**
**Motorola 1,568.9%       Hormel Foods 5,946.6%**
Source: Center for Security Prices, University of Chicago

# CHAPTER EIGHT

lyst or money manager can experience when arriving at the need to select individual stocks. That is one reason why the S&P 500 outperforms approximately 60% of all retail equity mutual funds to the present day!

Meanwhile, back at home port, Mr. Marmot explained to his sales peers that the lovely Jane Cromwell had invited him to visit her in "The Big Apple." Always one to impress, Caesar pointed out that there are more French restaurants in New York City than in Paris. He planned to dine at several. He was also compelled to expound a bit more trivia. "The first lighthouse to use electricity," he stated, "was the Statue of Liberty. In fact, the first mini golf courses were constructed in 1926 and resided on New York City rooftops. And, in 1895, the speed limit in New York City was a whopping eight miles per hour," Caesar lectured. Giving their full attention, his peers nodded appreciatively.

Broker Marmot was understandably beside himself after speaking on the telephone with Jane and, to his surprise, learning of her oblique acceptance of his plea to visit her and her associates in New York. He was unable to contain his jubilation. He announced to many of his broker peers the source of his obvious excitement. Noting that their response seemed underwhelming, Caesar chose to embellish the story a bit. He bragged to his fellow brokers that, while in New York City, he would get permission from Jane to invest the roughly $800,000 in cash that had accumulated from sales in her family trust. A breach of good faith? Absolutely! But Caesar Marmot was, after all, intellectually

## THE WALL STREET CASINO

challenged. (The closest he ever got to a 4.0 average in college was his blood alcohol content.)

Unfortunately, Mr. Marmot's colleagues had experienced his unusual wagering behavior before and challenged him to back up his bravado with a substantial wager that they would share against his providence. It seemed appropriate that the lunchroom radio was tuned to Valarie Pettiford singing "Big Spender." Over the next three quarters of an hour, the wagering elevated until at last his beloved (and partially paid for) yacht was on the bargaining table. By now, some sixteen fellow salespersons had taken on the adverse side of the wager and prodded him for even further concessions. Caesar was red-faced and noticeably nervous as he once again resorted to twirling the black hair on his neck mole. (These were not signs of great self-confidence.) Fortunately, for him, it was time to depart to the airport if he intended to make his flight to New York. (He could have wagered his home!)

"Up for grabs"

# CHAPTER EIGHT

# Notes

# ROBERT KNEISLEY

## Author's Comment

Looking toward our global economy today is looking toward uncertainty for Americans. Future demographics only heighten the suspense. As demographics continue to dictate an older class of American citizens, our majority rule politicians will continue to favor the older, majority voters. The result can well be an unbalanced favoritism toward members of AARP at the expense of future generations. It is critically important that parents educate their children with regard to investing their money to ensure a comfortable retirement.

This can be accomplished, I feel, by either investing funds under the gift to minors account status in passive index funds or by teaching the children to research those mutual funds and showing the children the resulting performance. This could be in the nature of a game that teaches our offspring to follow investments, whether they are stocks, bonds, or mutual funds and to understand the importance of compound interest and the destruction of compound interest if the child's allowance is expended for frivolous purposes.

Parents could also buy one share of some child-oriented stock and follow that stock to teach them. Parents and grandparents should also open tax-advantaged accounts for their children and grandchildren early in their life so that they can grow substantial assets to help them in the future. I am sure most grandparents and parents would agree that they would have benefited had their parents done so. It would appear that we must all reduce our dependence upon the government entitlement programs and fend for ourselves. That, of course, is a quality that built America.

# Chapter Nine

Once again, the excursionists were blessed with fine weather as they departed Vladivostok and began their journey through the north Pacific passage moving south, thence through the Panama Canal, Caribbean Sea, and then north to New York City. They entered the Atlantic Ocean destined for New York Bay. Presently, they could clearly see the glittering metropolis we know as New York City, the heart of commerce and the home of the "Wall Street Casino." Shortly, they would see the majestic Statue of Liberty as they moved up the East River. As the sun splashed off the East River, our trio proceeded up the watery canyon toward the very popular 79th Street Marina where *Aquarius* would be safely docked.

Adam was still in tour guide mode and began to explain that this magnificent city with a population of 17,846,000 people became absolutely deserted in the financial district after 6:00 p.m. He pointed out that many travel for over two hours to get to their offices and two hours back home in the evening. He pointed out that Warren Buffet stated that Wall Street was unique in the fact that people would travel in their Rolls Royces to obtain investment advice from people who arrived via the subway. They all laughed heartily at the reality of his statement.

The topography, he said, was ever changing as buildings were destroyed and recreated on a continuous basis. Their plan today, he said, was to travel by cab to Fraunce's Tavern, where the New York Stock Exchange and American Stock Exchange specialists and floor traders congregated after market hours. It was there that the trio would have the great privilege of visiting with Dr. William Shrill to discuss the inner workings of Wall Street from an academic point of view. To their surprise, upon hailing, a cab going in the opposite direction made a dramatic, high speed U-turn and stopped abruptly before the trio. Bryce opened the rear door so that Jane could enter, and Adam took the passenger seat. "Fraunce's Tavern, please," Bryce requested.

"Is okay!" responded the driver whom they suspected might be Italian.

Much conversation ensued as the passengers viewed all the typical New York City activity while their cab sped to the tavern. Upon their arrival, Bryce was careful to provide a sufficient tip to the driver, having had past experiences that illuminated the sensitivity and colorful language of some New York cabbies.

As they entered the ancient tavern, there seemed to be quiet recognition of Adam Smith's presence by some of the Wall Street crowd at the bar and at many of the tables.

# CHAPTER NINE

An ominous quiet developed as the trio made their way to the Washington Room and took a seat to await the arrival of Dr. Shrill. "You are in the company of great history here," remarked Adam as he engaged Jane in conversation. "Sam Fraunce purchased this building in 1762, and early on, it became a very popular tavern. The tavern was frequented by many leaders of the Revolutionary War and was more than just a local watering hole.

Fraunce's Tavern

"Mind you, I recall that in the eighteenth century, taverns were the newspapers of today. This is where people would meet to do business and to interact socially and where everyone got the latest news. At that time, it was news about the growing political unrest in the colonies. This is where, in 1768, the New York Chamber of Commerce was born. It is also where the Sons of Liberty galvanized support for the coming Revolution. In fact, it was here that the provincial Congress of New York held meetings and Sam Fraunce first met the father of our country, George Washington. Their friendship led to Fraunce's appointment as Chief Steward in our first president's household. I hope that explains why Bryce and I thought that you would be most comfortable in this, the Washington Room."

Suddenly, both Bryce and Adam held up their hands in the direction of the entranceway as if to shield their faces from radiation. The gesture soon morphed into a weak wave as attorney Reggie Rasmussen entered the Washington Room with a loud "hello!" aimed at the trio. Jane realized immediately that Mr. Rasmussen was somewhat less than a popular acquaintance. He was a short fellow with a mismatched sport jacket and a stale coffee stain on his white shirt. He referred to Adam as "old man" as he slapped him vigorously on the back. He turned and shook hands with Bryce and gave a suggestive wink to Jane. Bryce introduced Reggie to Jane but did not invite him to be seated.

It should be noted here that Mr. Rasmussen was a very wealthy attorney noted for his defense of major players on Wall Street. In spite of his oath, he also served as a clearinghouse for legal information transfer between firms and their employees. Street wise and ruthless, he was a character well ensconced in the "Wall Street casino" "How's tricks?" Mr. Rasmussen inquired.

"Just fine. We are here to introduce Ms. Cromwell to the vagaries of the street," responded Bryce with a smile.

"Vagaries? That's my business! How may I be of assistance to you, Ms. Cromwell?" asked Mr. Rasmussen.

Jane was puzzled for an instant and then responded, "Is there a great need for an attorney in what is commonly referred to as the citadel of capitalism?" she inquired.

"Need? I'm the oil that lubricates progress on Wall Street. Without legal representation, most respected financial firms in the citadel would have expired many decades ago."

"I find that hard to believe. I think most people hold Wall Street institutions in very high regard," Jane said.

# CHAPTER NINE

"Yes. That's because of my work," Mr. Rasmussen humbly retorted.

At this point Bryce noticed that Professor Shrill had entered the tavern, and Bryce was eager to dismiss the exorable Mr. Rasmussen. "I'm sorry, Reggie, to interrupt but our guest has arrived. Could you please excuse us?" Bryce said politely.

"I get your drift, Cunningham. Ms. Cromwell, in order to save time, I would suggest you read the Securities and Exchange Commission Web site news releases to get an idea about how busy we attorneys have been and the major settlements these *respected institutions* have had to pay. We're talking billions of dollars here!"

Slapping Bryce and Adam briskly on the back and waving adieu to Jane, Mr. Rasmussen departed.

Jane made a mental note to review the SEC site posthaste. (You can review 2007–2008 major settlements in Table One at the end of this chapter.) Bryce later suggested that Jane should also review a book entitled *Wall Street Versus America* by Gary Weiss for more insider detail concerning how the "casino" operates. She promised to do so.

Dr. Shrill visited with several individuals in the main entrance area before proceeding to the Washington Room where he was warmly greeted by Bryce and Adam. They introduced Dr. Shrill to Jane and proceeded to explain that Dr. Shrill's research had been critical in the expansion and acceptance of academia's Modern Portfolio Theory and a means to control volatility as measured by standard deviation in portfolios. An Ivy League professor, Dr. Shrill's eloquence matched his stately appearance. He was about six feet in height with an athletic build and was about sixty years of age.

Pleasantries were exchanged for a few minutes, and Dr. Shrill ordered a glass of wine. Bryce explained that Dr. Shrill won a Nobel Prize for developing a better way to compare return with overall market measures. After a verbal spiral of explanation, Jane appeared to be even more puzzled with Bryce's comments. Adam Smith interjected. "Jane, many of the more scientific comparisons of portfolio return tend to fail to consider the risk factor. A raw return figure should always require further analysis because investors need to know how the portfolio has performed *in relation to the market in general as well as relative to other portfolios*. There exist many risk-adjusted and market-adjusted rate-of-return measures regarding the assessment of portfolio performance. Dr. Shrill will explain his most favorite—the Sharpe's measure. Dr. Shrill you have the floor, sir."

Dr. Shrill looked intently at Jane as he stated, "Jane, Dr. William Sharpe of Dartmouth won a Nobel Prize for his development of what is known today as Sharpe's measure. By simply dividing the total portfolio return minus the current interest rate of a treasury bill by the portfolio standard deviation or volatility, an investor can assess the *risk premium* of one's portfolio."

Jane was about to engage Dr. Shrill in a deeper explanation when she noted an old friend approaching with what

## CHAPTER NINE

appeared to be another stockbroker. It was the now infamous Caesar Marmot! The other party was unnamed and unidentifiable. However, Caesar would soon unflappably correct that assumption. Raising both arms in male surrender, Caesar screamed, "Jane! I made it!" as he dragged his sorry self in her direction, threw his arms around her, and delivered a robust kiss to her lips.

She resisted, noting that Caesar reeked of alcohol. Jane blushed with embarrassment as she introduced Caesar Marmot to the table members and then inquired as to his friend.

"I have had the extreme pleasure of imbibing all afternoon with this gentleman, Mr. Graven Wellstock of Wellstock, Figby & Prentice, LLC. Graven is the founder and CEO of that elite full service brokerage firm soon to be a legend on Wall Street!" bellowed Caesar, and the introductions resounded in kind around the table.

Bryce, sensing the opportunity for instant (if not colorful) education for Jane, invited the stockbrokers to join them and order a cocktail. Dr. Shrill commented that he recalled that Wellstock, Figby & Prentice underwrote several proprietary mutual funds. Mr. Wellstock confirmed that fact and explained that the funds were a very lucrative source of cash flow. When Adam inquired as to the performance since inception, he learned that, even with the most positive spin Mr. Wellstock could generate, the funds, like most retail brokered funds, underperformed the leading indexes. Adam then asked Mr. Wellstock how they trained their stockbrokers regarding the history of finance.

"Mr. Smith, we are not a community college. We are a brokerage firm, and we hire sales professionals or, if not, we train our brokers to be sales professionals."

"Indeed?" said Mr. Smith with a smile. "And, Mr. Marmot, we understand that you have been in the brokerage industry for well over a decade. How much financial history education does your training include?"

"Our firm carefully screens every candidate. The screening actually includes psychological testing to be certain that we have the attributes to go through the training here on Wall Street that, I understand, is equivalent to a master's degree in finance! I am trained to select stocks based upon our analyst's recommendation rankings," Caesar responded with a smile.

"You're begging the question, young man," Adam challenged. "The question pertained to the study of the history of financial matters. Was that a topic in your training?"

Caesar seemed overly sensitive to what he felt was, in fact, a reprimand from Mr. Smith. With eyes lowered to the table, he responded that the training his firm provided focused more on investor sales psychology and product reviews. He volunteered that much of the study text featured not so much the history of finance as the history of very successful sales professionals.

It was Bryce's turn to administer the lash. He addressed Caesar with a smile and inquired as to the profit his firm earned from the *marketing fees* paid to position various mu-

# CHAPTER NINE

tual fund families for sale by his retail brokerage firm. Caesar was apparently blindsided by the question. Upon further interrogation, it was obvious that he had absolutely no knowledge of the fact that his employer was collecting fees in addition to the commissions that they received. That conversation led into how both firms selected money managers to present to their clients in the form of "wrap fee"[9] accounts. Mr. Wellstock presented an obvious fog of information that totally evaded the question. Caesar was more forthcoming. He had absolutely no idea… and said as much.

Dr. Shrill stroked his chin thoughtfully as he asked Mr. Wellstock how many pages were included in his mutual fund's "Statement of Additional Information."

"I believe you mean 'prospectus,'" interjected Caesar.

A brief silence occurred as everyone realized that Mr. Marmot was not at all familiar with the term. "Au contraire," Dr. Shrill responded. "We are familiar with the fact that each mutual fund, by law, must distribute a prospectus to an investor who acquires shares of the fund. Unfortunately, the prospectus usually arrives with the statement after the trade is consummated. While we disagree with that procedure, it is legal. What I am referring to, however, is a document that most brokers are unfamiliar with because their broker/dealer elects not to tell them about the Statement of Additional Information that illuminates additional fees and charges.

"Might I suggest to you, Mr. Marmot, that you discuss and even review the Statement of Additional Information

---

[9] A charge for an investment management program that bundles together a suite of services such as brokerage, advisory, research, and management.

concerning the Wellstock proprietary mutual funds? I think you might find it very enlightening. I further think you owe it to your investing clients to understand, in more depth, the products you are selling...and their costs."

Caesar was crestfallen and humiliated.

Mr. Wellstock finally seemed to understand where this conversational trail might end and politely excused himself, retiring to the main lounge. Bryce was completely aware of what was going on with Jane's trust account and inquired of Caesar regarding his methodology for asset allocation. Laughing, Caesar said, as his mind danced through lyrics from "The Good, the Bad and the Ugly," "I follow the Will Rogers theory of investing; I try to buy stocks that go up. And, if they don't, I don't buy 'em!" Caesar was once again nervously twisting his mole hair in an attempt to nullify his frustration. The torture, however, was not over.

Bryce asked Caesar if he had ever sold any of Wellstock's mutual funds, and Caesar responded that he had. Bryce asked if he had explained the *expense ratio* that outlines a portion of the internal cost of the fund to his investors. "The law requires that they receive a prospectus and we make certain that they do!" snapped Caesar as he abruptly rose, knocking his chair to the floor, and departed angrily.

Jane raised her hands as if to say "good riddance!" and all seemed to agree that the repartee was not simply entertaining but was an educational benefit for Jane.

# CHAPTER NINE

# Table One

## S.E.C. Legal Settlements January, 2007–April, 2008

| Date | Subject Case | Case No. | Settlement Amount |
|---|---|---|---|
| 4/25/2008 | RS Investments | 34-56222 | $30 Million |
| 3/5/2008 | Fidelity Investments | N/A | $8 Million |
| 1/18/2007 | Fred Alger Management | 34-55118 | $40 Million |
| 1/29/2007 | MBIA Inc. | 33-8776 | $50 Million |
| 2/6/2007 | RenaissanceRe Holdings Ltd. | N/A | $15 Million |
| 4/14/2007 | Goldman Sachs Group, Inc. | 34-55465 | $2 Million |
| 4/14/2007 | Banc of America Securities, LLC | 34-55466 | $26 Million |
| 4/21/2007 | Veras Hedge Funds | 34-54299 | $38 Million |
| 4/23/2007 | PBHG Funds | 34-54812 | $125 Million |
| 4/26/2007 | Edward D. Jones & Co. L.P. | 34-53660 | $79 Million |
| 4/30/2007 | Fannie Mae | N/A | $357 Million |
| 5/2/2007 | A.G. Edwards and Sons | 34-55692 | $3.86 Million |
| 5/7/2007 | Zurich Capital Markets | 34-55711 | $16.8 Million |
| 5/9/2007 | Morgan Stanley & Co. | 34-55726 | $7.9 Million |
| 5/23/2007 | BISYS | N/A | $25 Million |

# THE WALL STREET CASINO

| 7/2/2007 | Columbia Funds | N/A | $37 Million |
|---|---|---|---|
| 8/7/2007 | BanCorp | N/A | $8.5 Million |
| 8/9/2007 | General American Life | 33-8832 | $3.3 Million |
| 8/13/2007 | Banc One Mutual Funds | N/A | $55.6 Million |
| 9/12/2007 | PBHG Funds | 34-54812 | $267 Million |
| 9/19/2007 | Evergreen Investment Management | 34-56462 | $32.5 Million |
| 9/27/2007 | Freddie Mac | 33-8850 | $50 Million |
| 10/10/2007 | Sandell Asset Management Corp. | 33-8857 | $8 Million |
| 10/19/2007 | Fannie Mae | N/A | $356 Million |
| 11/20/2007 | Massachusetts Financial Services | 34-56122 | $31.5 Million |

# CHAPTER NINE

# Notes

# THE WALL STREET CASINO

## Author's Comment

*What is passive investing anyway? The approach presumes that markets are efficient. University of Chicago Finance Professor Eugene F. Fama provides the best description of his Efficient Market Hypothesis. He stated that "...In an efficient market at any point in time, the actual price of a security will be a good estimate of its intrinsic value."*

*Passive investing involves the engineering of a portfolio of properly allocated "baskets" of securities that either mimic or replicate indexes. That is to say that one could purchase each stock that makes up the Dow Jones Industrial Average thus replicating the Dow Jones index. While that method is effective, I do not feel that this type of index investing is nearly as effective as asset class index fund investing. The best system our research has determined does indeed involve asset class index portfolio allocations with portfolio rebalancing as needed. The advantages listed below can be critical to your investment success.*

### Passive Advantages Include

- ☑ *Minimal Capital Gains Tax*
- ☑ *Low Expense Ratios*
- ☑ *Low Turnover*
- ☑ *Low Trading Costs (if any)*
- ☑ *No Sales Commissions*
- ☑ *No "Style Drift"*
- ☑ *Automatic Rebalancing*
- ☑ *No Speculation—No Surprises*

# CHAPTER NINE

### The Asset Class Investment Portfolio Process

*The investor must first determine the dimensions of risk/return that are desired and then select securities that are negatively correlated. Then, one determines the proper balance between two broad categories: stocks and bonds.*

*Further refinement includes determining the amount to invest in large versus small capitalization stocks within the portfolio, and lastly, the levels of value stocks versus growth stocks and the amount of international coverage desired.*

*Be aware that the original balance of the above must be maintained because all markets are dynamic, and the balances can change very quickly over time. If you feel this process is complicated, you are very perceptive. It is complicated and requires diligent attention to detail and the need for rebalancing to be successful.*

*Many highly qualified <u>fee-only</u> advisors can help you with the process. Please seek out such a firm and continue learning about this highly successful long-term investment process.*

# THE WALL STREET CASINO

# Chapter Ten

Caesar bolted out of Fraunce's Tavern in a rage, hailed a cab, and planned his revenge as he traveled toward the East River and *Aquarius*. Upon arriving at the assigned dock, the dock master waved a friendly hello as Caesar approached the berth where *Aquarius* was tethered. Boarding the vessel he, not surprisingly, found the salon door unlocked and entered with a plan. Realizing that time was precious, Caesar searched the salon and state rooms for a portable sound system speaker. He thought to himself how fortunate it was that he too was a boater and realized the magnetic sensitivity of the compass at the helm of *Aquarius*.

At that precise instant, he realized that he had lost his wager with his office peers! (He was no longer the owner of his yacht...and no longer a boater.) His smoldering rage now burst into all consuming flame! He located a shelf speaker in the second stateroom. He raced to the bridge, opened the locker next to the compass, and placed the speaker as close to the compass as possible. Caesar realized that the huge magnet in the speaker would distract the compass several degrees. He also realized that the global positioning and all other directional instrumentation on *Aquarius* were networked so that the compass controlled the ultimate direction of the vessel. He felt that if he could not have Jane and retain her respect, then no one else should! He wished the entire party would meet with a sea disaster and perish in hell.

The targets of his rage returned to *Aquarius* an hour later, prepared the yacht, and cast off for their northern trip to the St. Lawrence Seaway and the friendly waters of Lake Erie on their return trip to Toledo. Jane retired once again to the salon, joining Mr. Smith. While the vessel moved in compressed time, Jane noted that Adam had poured his traditional beverage as he exclaimed, "Aye! What a fine educational meeting that was! Jane, I salute you." Raising his glass, and Jane, her traditional tea, Adam proposed a toast to her. "May her heart be light and happy, her smile big and wide, and may her pockets always have a coin or two inside!"

Suddenly, *Aquarius* shuddered violently and then stopped abruptly, throwing Jane's head against a bulkhead. Mr. Smith slid thirty feet forward through a companionway striking a bulkhead near the bow and Captain Bryce was catapulted through the vinyl bridge screens and fifteen feet forward on the deck. They had run aground at Cape Sable!

# CHAPTER TEN

Bryce rose almost immediately and realized that he was bruised and sore, but not severely injured. He moved around the gunwale on the starboard side of the vessel toward the aft deck and entered the salon. He saw that Jane was unconscious and examined her bleeding head while laying her on a nearby couch. Through his tears, he noticed that she was still breathing and felt encouraged as he went to determine Adam Smith's condition. Adam, however, was gone!

Bryce tended to Jane's wounds and placed ice on her injured head. He then radioed the Coast Guard for assistance. The Coast Guard arrived within the hour and immediately transferred Jane to a hospital in Halifax, Nova Scotia. They also helped Bryce solidly anchor *Aquarius* in anticipation of a rising tide and then transported him to the hospital to care for Jane.

Bryce spent the evening and the following day waiting for Jane to regain consciousness. He received periodic reports from the hospital physicians. They explained that the coma could last for days or even weeks. As Bryce sat praying and waiting in Jane's hospital room, one could almost hear the sad drone of a viola punctuating an ominous tragedy.

It was thirty-six long hours before Jane regained consciousness. She seemed now to have a hazy recollection of her trip to work, the screeching of tires, and the shattering of the windshield. Still dazed, she asked, "How is Adam?" with obvious effort.

## THE WALL STREET CASINO

"Adam? Who is Adam?" Bryce inquired.

Jane was perplexed. "Adam Smith, your partner!" Jane stammered with wonder.

Bryce gently embraced Jane and advised her that she had suffered a severe head injury when she drove her car left of center and was struck by another vehicle. He explained that the physician suggested that she may have a concussion and that her condition could have led to hallucination.

She recounted her long voyage and the experiences along the way. Bryce suggested that she did indeed have a concussion as evidenced by her account of the voyages. Jane now realized that her wonderful excursion experience with Bryce and Adam Smith was only a coma-induced hallucination and thanked the Lord for her survival.

Bryce stayed with Jane over the next week and over the course of time, explained that the market correction she imagined did occur but that he had been in contact with Jane's mother who had permitted the family's portfolio to be restructured in Bryce's care...and in passive investments that had withstood the test of time with very modest losses. More importantly, Bryce explained, her mother was alive and well.

Bryce and Jane have been married now for more than a year. Caesar Marmot was invited, but he did not attend their wedding. He ultimately met with severe financial distress and left the city. It seems only Adam Smith's memory remains with us. Or, might we have retained some sound

# CHAPTER TEN

investment knowledge? You can be certain that Adam would have wished it so.

## -The End-

# THE WALL STREET CASINO

# CHAPTER TEN

# Appendix One

## Unbridled Greed and Government Complacency?

The selfish, self-serving attitude of suspected crude oil speculators and the debilitating economic loss to the American economy that they may have created is without parallel. We pray that those that were in command at the Commodities Futures Trading Commission (CFTC) or elsewhere will receive just punishment if speculation and the violation of law are proven.

The dramatic increase in gasoline cost worldwide led our firm (along with hundreds of other financial industry firms, I'm sure) to request information regarding potential speculation in crude oil futures. While doing so might seem an easy task, it simply led to a bureaucratic vacuum. Please note the following chronology and the disarming lack of response to us humble taxpayers. The ultimate refusal to provide information was sent on August 6, 2008. Please refer to the document copies below.

# THE WALL STREET CASINO

Release: 5508-08
For Release: June 10, 2008

## CFTC Announces Interagency Task Force to Study Commodity Markets

Washington, DC – In light of the recent rise in crude oil and other commodity prices and the influx of new investors into commodity futures markets, the Commodity Futures Trading Commission (CFTC) is announcing the formation of an interagency task force to evaluate developments in commodity markets. The task force – which includes staff representatives from the CFTC, the Federal Reserve, the Department of the Treasury, the Securities and Exchange Commission, the Department of Energy, and the Department of Agriculture – will examine investor practices, fundamental supply and demand factors, and study the role of speculators and index traders in the commodity markets.

High commodity prices are posing a significant strain on U.S. households and the announced Interagency Task Force will aid public and regulatory understanding of the forces that are affecting the functioning of these markets. The Interagency Task Force will strive to complete its work as expeditiously as possible, and will make public the results.

Last Updated: June 10, 2008

### Robert Kneisley

From: Robert Kneisley [wealth@indicatoradvisory.com]
Sent: Monday, June 16, 2008 10:41 AM
To: 'enforcement@sec.gov'
Subject: Low margin requirements for oil futures contracts

We understand that the margin requirement for oil futures contracts is only 14%. Such a low investment level could invite speculation if several countries producing oil were to band together a year or two ago to control pricing. Has the SEC made any effort to investigate or to raise the minimum margin level? Can profits from our own Strategic Petroleum Reserves be used to counteract such activity by selling contracts short?

Please advise.

Sincerely,

Bob Kneisley


Release: 5517-08
For Release: July 9, 2008

## CFTC Announces Appointment of Stephen J. Obie as Acting Director of the Division of Enforcement

Washington, DC – The Commodity Futures Trading Commission (CFTC or Commission) announced today the appointment of Stephen J. Obie as Acting Director of the Division of Enforcement, effective immediately. Obie is currently the Regional Counsel/Associate Director and Regional Administrator for the CFTC's New York Office.

"In his time with the Commission, Steve Obie has worked on a broad range of investigations and enforcement actions involving our energy markets, including those brought against Enron, Dynegy Marketing and Trade, American Electric Power Company, Inc., The Williams Companies, and Amaranth," said CFTC Acting Chairman Walt Lukken. "He has a big role to fill and I am confident he is up to the challenge. I appreciate his service and look forward to continuing to work with him in this new capacity."

Obie joined the Commission in 1998 as a Senior Trial Attorney in the New York Office of the Division of Enforcement. Obie received his law degree, cum laude, in 1991 from the State University of New York at Buffalo School of Law and his B.A., summa cum laude, from Drew University. After law school, he clerked for the Hon. Jerome F. Hanifin of the NYS Court of Claims and at the Office of the Staff Attorneys for the US Court of Appeals for the Eighth Circuit. Prior to joining the CFTC in 1998, Obie was a litigator at Fried Frank Harris Shriver & Jacobson. Obie was an associate adjunct faculty member at Brooklyn Law School for the Fall 2007 semester, teaching an upper class seminar entitled "Trading Derivatives."

Last Updated: July 9, 2008

# THE WALL STREET CASINO

### Robert Kneisley

**From:** "Robert Kneisley" <wealth@indicatoradvisory.com>
**To:** <questions@cftc.gov>
**Sent:** Monday, July 14, 2008 9:37 AM
**Subject:** OIG: report fraud, waste and abuse at CFTC

Dear Sir or Madam:

It has come to our attention that margin requirements for crude oil contracts are only 14%. Is that true?

If so, it occurs to us that such a minimal investment level might have invited increased price control if several producing nations had banded together two years ago to control pricing. The estimate to accomplish that goal is as low as $200,000.000.

May we suggest that profits from our own Strategic Petroleum Reserves purchased years ago at much lower cost, be applied to counteract such activity by simply selling short crude contracts to lower the price? How might you implement such a program in a level-handed fashion?

We contacted the SEC Office of Enforcement on this question on June 16, 2008. Upon follow-up by telephone we were advised that they had no record of our email. We hope that your response might be more timely. Please feel free to call us if you have questions.

Bob Kneisley

# ON JULY 15TH THROUGH JULY 16TH, OIL PRICES DROPPED MORE THAN $10.50 PER BARREL!

# THE WALL STREET CASINO

**Robert Kneisley**

**From:** "Robert Kneisley" <wealth@indicatoradvisory.com>
**Sent:** Friday, July 18, 2008 2:00 PM
**Subject:** Fw: report fraud, waste and abuse at CFTC

----- Original Message -----
**From:** Robert Kneisley
**To:** questions@cftc.gov
**Sent:** Monday, July 14, 2008 9:40 AM
**Subject:** OIG: report fraud, waste and abuse at CFTC

Dear Sir or Madam: SECOND REQUEST

It has come to our attention that margin requirements for crude oil contracts are only 14%. Is that true?

If so, it occurs to us that such a minimal investment level might have invited increased price control if several producing nations had banded together two years ago to control pricing. The estimate to accomplish that goal is as low as $200,000,000.00!

May we suggest that profits from our own Strategic Petroleum Reserves purchased years ago at much lower cost, be applied to counteract such activity by simply selling short crude contracts to lower the price? How might you implement such a program in a level-handed fashion?

We contacted the SEC Office of Enforcement on this question on June 16, 2008. Upon follow-up by telephone we were advised that they had no record of our email. We hope that your response might be more timely.

OUR ORIGINAL EMAIL TO YOU WAS ON JULY 14TH. PLEASE FAVOR US WITH YOUR RESPONSE. Please feel free to call us if you have questions.

INDICATOR ADVISORY CORPORATION

Bob Kneisley

## Wednesday, August 6, 2008

**From:** Easter, Stacy [mailto:seaster@CFTC.gov]
**Sent:** Wednesday, August 06, 2008 1:23 PM
**To:** wealth@indicatoradvisory.com
**Subject:** CFTC FOIA NO. 08-0122

Mr. Kneisley:

This e-mail is in final response to your July 23, 2008 Freedom of Information Act request regarding crude oil contracts.

Commission staff has identified material responsive to your request and has determined that your request should be denied in total. The material is being withheld pursuant to exemption 3 of the Freedom of Information Act, 5 U.S.C. § 552(b)(3), pertaining to material specifically exempted from disclosure by statute (Section 8(a) of the Commodity Exchange Act, 7 U.S.C. § 12 which states that the Commission "may not publish data and information that would separately disclose the business transactions or market positions of any person.

You may, if you wish, file an appeal for access to information denied you by this letter. Your appeal must be filed within 30 days of the date of this letter. Your appeal must be in writing and must contain a statement of the grounds upon which you are basing your appeal. Please refer to the FOIA number that has been assigned to this request (FOIA No. 08-0122). Your appeal should be addressed: Freedom of Information Act Appeal, Office of the General Counsel, Commodity Futures Trading Commission, Three Lafayette Centre, 8th Floor, 1155 - 21st Street, N.W., Washington, D.C. 20581. Please send a copy of your appeal to the FOIA Compliance Office, Commodity Futures Trading Commission, Three Lafayette Centre, 8th Floor, 1155 - 21st Street, N.W., Washington, D.C. 20581. Questions concerning the processing of an appeal should be directed to the Office of the General Counsel at (202) 418-5120.

Please direct any questions you may have concerning the initial processing of your request to me.

Sincerely,

Stacy J. Easter
Paralegal Specialist
CFTC - OGC/ FOIA Compliance Office
1155 21st Street, NW
Washington, DC 20581
202-418-5011 (office)
202-418-5124 (fax)

# THE WALL STREET CASINO

**Attorney General**
*Andrew M. Cuomo*

Home | Contact Us | Site Index | En español       Search

- About Andrew Cuomo
- Tour the AG's Office
- Press Releases
- Family
- Communities
- Public Institutions
- Employment
- Service
- Procurement
- Opinions
- Links to Other Sites
- NYS Government

Thank You
Office of the New York State Attorney General Andrew M. Cuomo

Thank You. The following information has been submitted:

Form submitted on Fri Aug 22 05:31:29 2008

Personal Information:
Mr Bob Kneisley
3061 Shoreland Avenue
Toledo, OH 43611
Phone: ###-###-####
Email: wealth@indicatoradvisory.com

Comments:
Dear Mr. Cuomo:

I understand that the margin requirement for crude oil contracts on the CFTC is only 14%! It has been suggested that as little investment as $200,000,000 by oil producing countries could have cornered the market two years ago. The result would contribute to the oil price increases we have witnessed.

I have contacted the CFTC and the New York Mercantile Exchange to no avail. Can you investigate this alongside your ARS investigation?

Please confirm receipt of this email. Your early resonse would be very much appreciated.

Sincerely,

Bob Kneisley

**ON SEPTEMBER 11, 2008, MAJOR NEWSPAPERS ANNOUNCED A REPORT BY MASTERS CAPITAL MANAGEMENT OUTLINING HOW $60 BILLION WORTH OF SPECULATIVE INVESTMENT DROVE THE PRICE OF CRUDE TO $145 PER BARREL!**

## The Present Investor Conundrum

"I'm from the government… and I want to help."

We have the most productive political system on the planet. That said, our system often elevates poorly qualified candidates to ever-higher office as they (or even their relatives of the same name) gain name recognition and funding.

Recent history has demonstrated that the above headline should ring fear into the hearts of our citizens. In the last analysis, our elected leadership has presently placed all investors in a quandary. Let's review as of July, 2008:

- *The advent of* adjustable rate mortgages. *In the early '80s, transferred much of the risk from the banking system to the shoulders of the mortgagee and led to less responsible borrowing.*

- *The* sub-prime mess *was born of too loose regulation, combined with Wall Street greed and enabling bankers/brokers.*

- *The development of biofuels resulted in a too acidic fuel that could not be transported within a pipeline. The result has delayed the proper focus on energy alternatives while raising food costs and spurring massive inflation.*

- *The much talked about "environmental problems" that are rooted in poor regulation over many decades.*

- *Gasoline cost has inflated well beyond supply/demand ratios according to the experts. While it has not yet been proven, there is strong suspicion that the CFTC or New York Mercantile Exchange had permitted too much leverage for commodity speculators. Further, it has been suggested that a few years ago, as little as $200 million could have "cornered" the crude oil markets by world producers. We e-mailed our concerns under the Freedom of Information Act to the Enforcement Division at the Security & Exchange Commission on June 16, 2008 and the CFTC on July 14, and July 18, 2008. We received an e-mail response from the SEC on August 7, 2008 indicating that we should contact the CFTC. Coincidentally, on July 9, 2008, the CFTC announced that they had appointed Stephen J. Obie as Acting Director of the Division of Enforcement. Two days later, the CFTC announced the formation of an interagency taskforce to evaluate developments in commodity markets, and on July 15, 2008, oil began its decline with a drop of $7 per barrel.*
- The lack of "War Bond" financing to fund our present two wars has led to extreme deficits, a weak dollar, added inflationary pressure, and confusion over public support.
- MarketBrowser.com reveals that M-2 money supply was $3.7 trillion in the mid-1990s. (M-2 is a key indicator of inflationary pressure.) By early 2008, M-2 had exploded by $3.9 trillion to $7.6 trillion! Look to the Federal Reserve for answers to such growth… and the expected higher inflation that will surely follow.

## THE WALL STREET CASINO

- On July 15, 2008, the dollar hit a new low against the Euro. Inflation was the highest in twenty years.
- Bear market Exchange Traded Funds growth up $7.4 billion at 2007 year end.
- A mortgage crisis witnessing foreclosures soaring 120% in the second quarter, 2008 (a total of 739,714 foreclosures in the second quarter).

...Just to name a few.

### What Can We Do?

The good news—today, political, business, and educational candidates can have all critical qualifications underpinned by the AllCan.org self-screening process to help minimize the traditional hype and innuendo that results in poorly focused voters unable to make rational decisions.

History is replete with politicians gone astray. Considering our present plight, might it be wise for us to insist that all candidates volunteer to "self-screen," identifying their qualifications, past history, accomplishments, and honest intentions? This can now be accomplished in a very straightforward, transparent manner on the Internet. Let's stop shooting ourselves in the foot. Let's encourage all candidates to adopt a higher standard!

# THE WALL STREET CASINO

## Non-Partisan Comments Concerning Our Present Circumstances

As of July 2008, we are confronted with the following dilemmas:
- A failed energy policy
- Unbalanced wealth transfer to the elderly
- Loss of our manufacturing base
- A divided Congress deadlocked on many difficult issues
- Debased public confidence
- Lack of a comprehensive immigration policy
- The Indemac Bank failure (90 banks on FDIC "Watch List" at present)

Furthermore, we understand that one-third of families with a single working spouse rank below the poverty level.

Might it finally be time to elect new political candidates that are better qualified at the outset? If you agree, insist that your candidate complete the voluntary "pre-screening" process online at www.allcan.org.

**ALLCAM.org**
Autonomous Launch Link to the Candidate Accreditation Network

A site in search of qualifying politicians and leaders willing to communicate with the public and willing to accept the benefits of doing so

# THE WALL STREET CASINO

## ...and our valuable heritage

Now that we have circumnavigated the globe briefly examining cultural highlights and capital formation differences, it should be evident that the most populous country in North America is also the country with the strongest capital formation capability. Five centuries have witnessed emigrants from all corners of the globe willing to endure the shortcomings of America of which we natives tend to complain.

Americans can be justly proud of their diversified, service-oriented economy and increasingly urban population. While our capitalistic and political system is far from perfect, we cannot help but love America.

# THE WALL STREET CASINO

## Investment success requires a solid economic foundation through improvement of our present regulatory/political system

Many years ago, a very successful "grassroots" series of workshops focused on political education in an effort to help citizens make better-informed voting decisions. These workshops were held neighbor-to-neighbor in homes throughout the land. The volunteer workshop leaders would be invited to attend area homes with a series of three or four pre-planned, informal programs that explained the political party structure from precinct committee members to presidential candidates. Light refreshments were served, and many visiting neighbors became lifelong friends. Such a non-partisan program is now being organized by our own Allcan.org.

If you have an interest in participating in the AllCan Workshop Series, please contact the AllCan Workshop Committee at askus@allcan.org. While you are there, why not pick a topic that interests you and take the opportunity to blog your thoughts? God bless you, and God bless America!

# Glossary of Investment Terms

**Active Management:** Applying projections of the economy along with fundamental and technical reasoning to attempt to outperform the market by owning mispriced securities.

**Alpha:** Measure of performance on a risk-adjusted basis.

**Annual Report:** A report that public companies are required to file annually that describes the preceding year's financial results and plans for the upcoming year. Annual reports include information about a company's assets, liabilities, earnings, profits, and other year-end statistics.

**Annuity:** A contract by which an insurance company agrees to make regular payments to someone for life or for a fixed period in exchange for a lump sum or periodic deposits.

**Asset Allocation:** The placement of a certain percentage of investment capital within different types of assets (e.g., 50% in stock, 30% in bonds, and 20% in cash).

**Asset Allocation Fund:** Mutual fund that holds varying percentages of stock, bonds, and cash within its portfolio.

**Asset Class Investing:** A *passive* investment management strategy employing multiple asset classes, i.e., stocks, bonds, cash, real estate, etc.

**Asset-weighted Returns:** Asset-weighted returns for a particular style category in a month are determined by calculating a weighted average return of all funds in that category in that particular month, with each fund's return being weighted by its total net assets. Asset-weighted returns are a better indicator of fund category performance measurement because they more accurately reflect the returns of the total money invested in that particular style category.

**Automatic Investment Plan:** An arrangement where investors agree to have money automatically withdrawn from a bank account on a regular basis to purchase stock or mutual fund shares.

**Automatic Reinvestment:** An option available to stock and mutual fund investors where fund dividends and capital gains distributions are automatically reinvested to buy additional shares and thereby increase holdings.

**Balanced Fund:** Mutual fund that holds bonds and/or preferred stock in a certain proportion to common stock in order to obtain both current income and long-term growth of principal.

**Basis Point:** One hundredth of one percent, as of interest rates, or investment yields.

**Bear Market:** Term used to describe a prolonged period of declining stock prices.

**Before (Pre)-tax Dollars:** Money contributed to a tax-deferred savings plan that you do not have to pay income tax on until withdrawal at a future date.

**Beta:** A measure of a stock's volatility; the average beta for all stocks is +1.

**Blue-chip Stock:** Term, derived from the most expensive chips in a poker game, used to indicate the stock of companies with long records of growth and profitability.

**Bond:** A debt instrument or IOU issued by corporations or units of government.

**Bond Fund:** Mutual fund that holds mainly municipal, corporate, and/or government bonds.

**Broker:** A professional who transfers investors' orders to buy and sell securities to the market and generally provides some financial advice.

**Broker/Dealer:** A firm that buys and sells mutual funds shares and other securities to and from investors.

**Bull Market:** Term used to describe a prolonged period of rising stock prices.

**Buy and Hold:** A strategy of purchasing an investment and keeping it for a number of years.

**Capital Appreciation:** An increase in market value of an investment (e.g., stock).

**Capital asset pricing model:** A model that describes the relationship between risk and expected return on a security.

**Capital Gains Distribution:** Payment to investors of profits realized upon the sale of securities.

**Capitalization:** The market value of a company, calculated by multiplying the number of shares outstanding by the price per share. Capitalization is often called "cap" for short in the names of specific investments (e.g., ABC Small Cap Growth Fund).

**Cash-value Life Insurance:** Type of life insurance contract that pays benefits upon the death of the insured and has a savings element that provides cash payments prior to death. (Use caution as values usually build too slowly.)

**Central Registration Depository (CRD):** A computerized system, which includes the employment, qualification, and disciplinary histories of more than 400,000 securities professionals who deal with the public. Consumers can get CRD information about a sales representative by calling (800)-289-9999 or visiting the Web site www.nasdr.com/2000.htm.

**Certificate of Deposit (CD):** An insured bank product that pays a fixed rate of interest (e.g., 5%) for a specified period of time.

**Certificate of Deposit Account Registry Service (CDARS):** Provides up to $50 million in FDIC insurance protection for savings.

**Churning:** When a broker excessively trades securities within an account for the purpose of increasing his or her commissions, rather than to further a client's investment goals.

**Class A Shares:** Mutual fund shares that incur a front-end sales charge upon purchase.

**Class B Shares:** Mutual fund shares that incur a back-end sales charge (also known as a contingent deferred sales charge or CDSC) if sold within five to six years of purchase.

**Class C Shares:** Mutual fund shares that incur higher management and marketing fees than Classes A and B, but no sales or redemption charges upon purchase or sale.

**Closed-end Fund:** An investment company that issues a limited number of shares that can be bought and sold on market exchanges.

**Cold Calling:** A practice used by salespeople of making unsolicited phone calls to people they do not know in order to attract new business.

**Collectible:** An investment in tangible items such as coins, stamps, art, antiques, and autographs.

**Commission:** Fee paid to a broker to trade securities, generally based on the number of shares traded (e.g., one hundred shares) or the dollar amount of the trade.

**Commodities:** An investment in a contract to buy or sell products such as fuel oil, pork, grain, coffee, sugar, and other consumer staple items by a specified future date.

**Common Stock:** Securities that represent a unit of ownership in a corporation.

**Composite Indices:** Stock market indices comprised of stocks traded on major stock exchanges: * *New York Stock Exchange Composite* (index of stocks traded on New York Stock Exchange), * *American Stock Exchange Composite* (index of stocks traded

## THE WALL STREET CASINO

on American Stock Exchange), * *NASDAQ Composite* (index of stocks traded over the counter in the quotation system of the National Association of Securities Dealers).

**Compound Interest:** Interest credited daily, monthly, quarterly, semiannually, or annually on both principal and previously credited interest.

**Convertible Securities:** Bonds or preferred stock that can be exchanged for a fixed number of shares of common stock in the same corporation.

**Core Holding:** The foundation of a portfolio (e.g., a stock index fund) to which an investor might add additional securities.

**Corporate Bonds:** Debt instruments issued by for-profit corporations.

**Direct Purchase Plans (DPPs):** *No load* stocks where every share, including the first, can be sold or purchased directly from a company without a broker.

**Discount Broker:** A broker that trades securities for a lower commission than a full-service broker does.

**Diversification:** The policy of spreading assets among different investments to reduce the risk of a decline in the overall portfolio from a decline in any one investment.

**Dividend:** A distribution of income from investments to shareholders.

**Dividend Reinvestment Plans (DRIPs):** Plans that allow investors to automatically reinvest any dividends a stock pays into additional shares.

**Dollar-cost Averaging:** Investing equal amounts of money (e.g., $50) at a regular time interval (e.g., quarterly) regardless of whether securities markets are moving up or down. This practice reduces average share costs to investors, who acquire more shares in periods of lower securities prices and fewer shares in periods of higher prices.

**Dow Jones Industrial Average:** The most widely used gauge of stock market performance. Also known as "The Dow," it tracks thirty stocks in large well-established U.S. companies.

**EDGAR (Electronic Data Gathering, Analysis, and Retrieval):** An electronic system developed by the U.S. Securities and Exchange Commission (SEC) that is used by companies to file documents required by the SEC for securities offerings and ongoing disclosure. EDGAR information is available to consumers on the Internet at **www.sec.gov**, usually within 24 hours after filing by a company. EDGAR information is also available in the SEC's public reference room by calling (202) 942-8090 or sending a fax to (202) 628-9001 or an e-mail to **publicreference@sec.gov**.

**Equal-weighted Returns:** Equal-weighted returns for a particular style category in a month are determined by calculating a simple average return of all funds in that category in that particular month.

**Equity Investing:** Becoming an owner or partial owner of a company or a piece of property through the purchase of investments such as stock, growth mutual funds, and real estate.

**Exchange-traded Fund (ETF):** An investment company, typically a mutual fund or unit investment trust, whose shares are traded intraday on stock exchanges at market-determined prices. Investors may buy or sell shares through a broker just as they would the shares of any publically traded company.

**Expense Ratio:** A fund's cost of doing business—disclosed in the prospectus—expressed as a percentage of its assets.

**Federal Deposit Insurance Corporation (FDIC):** Federal agency that insures bank deposits up to $100,000. Investments purchased at banks are not FDIC-insured.

**Fixed Annuity:** An investment vehicle often used for retirement accounts that guarantees principal and a specified interest rate. Fixed annuity earnings grow tax-deferred until withdrawal.

**401(k) Plan:** A retirement savings plan sponsored by for-profit companies that allows an employee to contribute pretax dollars to a company investment vehicle until the employee retires or leaves the company.

**403(b) Plan:** Similar to a 401(k), a retirement savings plan for employees of a tax-exempt education or research organization or public school. Pretax dollars are contributed to an investment account until the employee retires or terminates employment.

**Full-service Broker:** A broker that charges commissions

based on the type and amount of securities traded. Full-service brokers typically charge more than discount brokers charge but also provide services that are more extensive (e.g., research and personalized advice).

**GNMAs or Ginnie Maes:** An investment in a pool of mortgage securities backed by Government National Mortgage Association (GNMA).

**Goldman, Marshall Ph.D.:** Harvard University, 1961; Kathyrn Wasserman Davis Professor of Russian Economics (Emeritus), Wellesley College; Senior Scholar, Davis Center

**Growth Fund:** Mutual fund that invests in stocks exhibiting potential for capital appreciation.

**Growth Stocks:** Stock of companies that are expected to increase in value.

**Guaranteed Investment Contract (GIC):** Fixed-income investments offered in many tax-deferred employer retirement plans that guarantee a specific rate of return for a specific time period.

**Income Fund:** Mutual fund that invests in stocks or bonds with a high potential for current income, either interest or dividends.

**Income Stocks:** Stock of companies that expect to pay regular and relatively high (compared to growth stocks) dividends.

**Index:** An unmanaged collection of securities whose overall performance is used as an indication of stock market trends. An example of an index is the widely quoted Dow

Jones Industrial Average, which tracks the performance of thirty large company U.S. stocks.

**Index Fund:** Mutual fund that attempts to match the performance of a specified stock or bond market index by purchasing some or all of the securities that comprise the index.

**Indices:** A benchmark index provides an investment vehicle to compare and assess fund performance.

**Individual Retirement Account (IRA):** A retirement savings plan that allows individuals to save for retirement on a tax-deferred basis.

**Interest Rate Risk:** The risk that, as interest rates rise, the value of previously issued bonds will fall, resulting in a loss if they are sold prior to maturity.

**Investment Clubs:** Organizations of investors who meet and contribute money regularly toward the purchase of securities.

**Investment Grade Bond:** Bond rated with one of the top four grades by a rating service such as Moody's and Standard & Poor's, indicating a high level of creditworthiness.

**Investment Objective:** The goal (e.g., current income) of an investor or a mutual fund. Mutual fund objectives must be clearly stated in the prospectus.

**Keogh Plan:** A qualified retirement plan for self-employed individuals and their employees to which tax-deductible contributions up to a specified yearly limit can be made if the plan meets certain requirements of the Internal Revenue Code.

**Limit Order:** An order to buy or sell securities that specifies that a trade should be made only at a certain price or better.

**Liquidity:** The quality of an asset that permits it to be converted quickly into cash without a significant loss of value.

**Load:** A commission charged by the sponsor of a mutual fund upon the purchase or sale of shares.

**Management Fee:** The amount paid by mutual funds to their investment advisers.

**Marginal Tax Rate:** The rate you pay on the last (highest) dollar of personal or household (if married) earnings. Current federal marginal tax rates range from 15% to 39.6%.

**Market Order:** An order to buy or sell a stated amount (e.g., 100 shares) of a security at the best possible price at the time the order is received in the marketplace.

**Market Value:** The current price of an asset, as indicated by the most recent price at which it traded on the open market. If the most recent trade in ABC stock was at $25 for example, the market value of the stock is $25.

**Marmot:** A large ground squirrel; member of the rodent family.

**Maturity:** The date on which the principal amount of a bond, investment contract, or loan must be repaid.

**Microcap Stock:** Low priced stocks issued by the smallest of companies. Companies with low or "micro" capitalization typically have limited assets and a small total market value. Many microcap stocks trade in small volumes in the "over the counter" (OTC) market, with prices quoted on the OTC Bulletin Board or "Pink Sheets."

**Modern Protfolio Theory:** A theory that optimizes expected return based on a given level of risk.

**Money Market Mutual Fund:** A highly liquid mutual fund that invests in short-term obligations such as commercial paper, government securities, and certificates of deposit.

**Moody's Investors Service:** A rating agency that analyzes the credit quality of bonds and other securities.

**Mutual Fund:** An investment company that pools money from shareholders and invests in a variety of securities, including stocks, bonds, and money market securities.

**Net Asset Value:** The market value of a mutual fund's total assets, after deducting liabilities, divided by the number of shares outstanding.

**Net Worth:** The dollar value remaining when liabilities (what you owe) are subtracted from assets (what you own). Example: $200,000 of assets − $125,000 of debt = a $75,000 net worth.

**Online Investing:** The purchase of securities from brokerage firms via the Internet using a computer and modem.

**Open-end Fund:** An investment company that continually buys and sells shares to meet investor demand. It can have an unlimited number of investors or money in the fund.

**Passive Investment Management:** Holding of broadly diversified securities in an effort to provide "Free Market" investment returns.

# THE WALL STREET CASINO

**Pavlov:** Refers to Ivan Petrovich Pavlov, a Russian physiologist, psychologist, and physician.

**Penny Stocks:** Stocks that sell for $5 per share or less.

**Portfolio:** The combined holding of stocks, bonds, cash equivalents, or other assets by an individual or household, investment club, or institutional investor (e.g., mutual fund).

**Portfolio Manager:** A specialist employed by a mutual fund's advisor to invest the fund's assets in accordance with predetermined investment objectives.

**Portfolio Turnover:** A measure of the trading activity in a fund's investment portfolio—how often securities are bought and sold by a fund.

**Preferred Stock:** A type of stock that offers no ownership or voting rights and generally pays a fixed dividend to investors.

**Price/Earnings (P/E) Ratio:** The price of a stock divided by its earnings per share (e.g., $40 stock price divided by $2 of earnings per share = a P/E ratio of 20).

**Principal:** The original amount of money invested or borrowed, excluding any interest or dividends.

**Prospectus:** An official booklet that describes a mutual fund. It contains information as required by the U.S. Securities and Exchange Commission on topics such as the fund's investment objectives, investment restrictions, purchase and redemption policies, fees, and performance history.

**Quartiles:** The $p^{th}$ –percentile for a set of data is the value which is greater than or equal to p% of the data, but is less than or equal to (100 – p)% of the data. So, it is a value that divides the data into two parts: the lower p% of the values and the upper (100 – p)% of the values. The first quartile is the $75^{th}$ percentile, the value separating the elements of a population into the lower 75% and the upper 25%. The second quartile is the $50^{th}$ percentile, and the third quartile is the $25^{th}$ percentile. For fund category quartiles in a particular time horizon, the data used is the return of the largest share class of the fund net of fees, but excluding loads.

**Real Estate:** Land, permanent structures on land, and accompanying rights and privileges, such as crop or mineral rights.

**Real Estate Investment Trust (REIT):** A portfolio of real estate-related securities in which investors can purchase shares that trade on major stock exchanges.

**Real-time Quotes:** A requirement that trades in a NASDAQ (over the counter market) security be reported within ninety seconds of execution. Thus, information is current up to ninety seconds of the market, rather than typical quotes, which have a fifteen- or twenty-minute delay.

**Reciprocal Immunity:** A principle of taxation where state and local governments do not tax earnings on federal debt securities and the federal government does not tax earnings on state/local debt securities.

**Risk:** Exposure to loss of investment capital (i.e., amount of money invested).

**Risk Management:** Actions taken (e.g., purchase of insurance) to provide protection against catastrophic financial losses (e.g., disability and liability). Risk management is an important investing prerequisite.

**Sales Charge:** The amount charged to purchase mutual fund shares. The charge is added to the net asset value per share to determine the per share offering price.

**Savings Incentive Match Plan for Employees (SIMPLE Plans):** A tax-deferred retirement plan for owners and employees of small businesses that provides matching funds by the employer.

**Securities:** A term used to refer to stocks and bonds in general.

**Securities and Exchange Commission (SEC):** Federal agency created to administer the Securities Act of 1933. Statues administered by the SEC are designed to promote full public disclosure about investments and protect the investing public against fraudulent and manipulative practices in the securities markets.

**Securities Investor Protection Corporation (SIPC):** A nonprofit corporation that insures investors against the failure of brokerage firms, similar to the way that the Federal Deposit Insurance Corporation (FDIC) insures bank deposits. Coverage is limited to a maximum of $500,000 per account, but only up to $100,000 in cash. SIPC does not insure against market risk, however.

**Simplified Employee Pension (SEP):** A tax-deferred retirement plan for owners of small businesses and the self-employed.

**Standard & Poor's Corporation:** A rating agency that analyzes the credit quality of bonds and other securities.

**Standard & Poor's 500 Index:** An index that is widely replicated by stock index mutual funds. Also known as the S&P 500, it consists of 500 large U.S. companies.

**Statement of Additional Information:** The supplementary document to a prospectus that contains more detailed information about a mutual fund.

**Stock:** Security that represents a unit of ownership in a corporation.

**Substandard Grade (a.k.a. "Junk") Bond:** Bond rated below the top four grades by a rating service such as Moody's and Standard & Poor's. They generally provide a higher return than investment grade securities to compensate investors for an increased risk of default.

**Survivorship Bias:** Many funds might liquidate or merge during a period of study. Most of these occur because of continued poor performance by the fund. Therefore, if index returns were compared to fund returns using only surviving funds, the comparison would be biased in favor of the fund category. These reports remove this bias by (a) taking all available funds in that particular category as the investment opportunity set as the denominator for outperformance calculations, (b) explicitly showing the survivorship rate in each category, and (c) constructing peer average return series for each style box based on all available funds at that period of time.

**Tax Deferral:** Investments where taxes due on the amount invested and/or its earnings are postponed until funds are withdrawn, usually at retirement.

**Tax-exempt:** Investments (e.g., municipal bonds) where earnings are free from tax liability.

**Total Return:** The return on an investment including all current income (interest and dividends), plus any change (gain or loss) in the value of the asset.

**12(b)1 Fee:** A marketing fee levied on mutual fund shareholders to pay for advertising and distribution costs, as well as broker compensation.

**Unit Investment Trust (UIT):** An unmanaged portfolio of professionally selected securities that are held for a specified period of time.

**U.S. Treasury Securities:** Debt instruments issued by the federal government with varying maturities (bills, notes, and bonds).

**Value Stock:** A stock with a relatively low price compared to its historical earnings and the value of the issuing company's assets.

**Variable Annuity:** An annuity where the value fluctuates

based on the market performance of its underlying securities portfolio.

**Volatility:** The degree of price fluctuation associated with a given investment, interest rate, or market index. The more price fluctuation that is experienced, the greater the volatility.

**Zero-coupon Bonds:** Debt instruments issued by government or corporations at a steep discount from face value. Interest accrues each year, but it is not paid out until maturity.

Source: Rutgers University

# For Further Reading

If you would like to learn more about the academic research pertaining to portfolio management, consider these books and articles:

Adriaans, Pieter, and Dolf Zantinge. *Data Mining*. Harlow, Eng.: Addison Wesley Longman, 1996.

Agrawal, Rakesh, et al. "Mining Association Rules Between Sets of Items in Large Databases." Proceedings of the 1993 ACM SIGMOD Conference, Washington, D.C., May 1993.

———. "Modeling Multidimensional Databases." Research Report, IBM Almaden Research Center, San Jose, CA, 1997.

Agrawal, S., et al. "On the Computation of Multidimensional Aggregates." Proceedings of the 22nd VLDB Conference, Bombay, India, 1996.

Ang, James S., and Jess H. Chua. "Composite Measures for the Evaluation of Investment Performance." *Journal of Financial and Quantitative Analysis* 14(2) (1979): 361–384.

Balzer, Leslie A. "Measuring Investment Risk: A Review." *Journal of Investing* 3(3) (1994): 47–58.

Bawa, Vijay S. "Optimal Rules for Ordering Uncertain Prospects." *Journal of Financial Economics* 2(1) (1975): 95–121.

Bey, Roger P. "Estimating the Optimal Stochastic Dominance Efficient Set with a Mean-Semi Variance Algorithm." *Journal of Financial and Quantitative Analysis* 14(5) (1979): 1059–1070.

Bogle, John C. *The Little Book of Common Sense Investing.* New Jersey: Wiley, 2007.

Bookstaber, Richard, and Roger Clarke. "Problems in Evaluating the Performance of Portfolios with Options." *Financial Analyst Journal* 41(1)(1985): 48–62.

Boyce, William E., and Richard C. DiPrima. *Elementary Differential Equations, 5th ed.* New York: Wiley, 1986.

Brinson, Gary P., L. Randolph Hood, and Gilbert L. Beebower. "Determinants of Portfolio Performance." *Financial Analyst Journal*, July–August 1986: 39–44.

Cabena, Peter, et. al. *Discovering Data Mining: From Concept to Implementation.* Upper Saddle River, NJ: Prentice Hall, 1997.

Cavallo, Roger E., and George J. Klir. "Reconstructability Analysis of Multi-dimensional Relations: A Theoretical Basis for Computer-aided Determination of Acceptable System Models." *International Journal of General Systems* 5 (1979): 143–171.

Chen, Peng, and Sherman Hanna. "Small Stocks vs. Large Stocks: It's How Long You Hold That Counts." *The Journal of American Association of Individual Investors*, July 1999.

Christensen, Ronald. *Analysis of Variance, Design and Regression.* London: Chapman& Hall, 1996. Domash, Harry. Fire Your Stock Analyst. Upper Saddle River, NJ: Financial Times Prentice Hall, 2003.

Edelman, Ric. *The Lies About Money.* New York: Simon & Schuster, 2007.

———. *The New Rules of Money.* New York: HarperCollins, 1998.

———. *Ordinary People, Extraordinary Wealth.* New York: HarperCollins, 2000.

———. *The Truth About Money.* New York: HarperCollins, 1996.

Efron, Bradley. "The Efficiency of Logistic Regression Compared to Normal Discriminant Analysis." *Journal of the American Statistical Association* 70 (1975): 892–898.

Elton, Edwin, Martin J. Gruber, and Manfred W. Padberg. Simple Criteria for Optimal Portfolio Selection. *Journal of Finance* 31(5) (1976):1341–1357.

Elton, Edwin, Martin J. Gruber, and Thomas Urich. Are Betas Best? *Journal of Finance* 33 (1978): 1375–1384.

Fama, Eugene F., and Kenneth R. French. The Cross Section of Expected Stock Returns. *Journal of Finance* 47(2) (1992): 427–466.

Fayyad, Usama M. Editorial. Data Mining and Knowledge *Discovery* 1 (1997): 5–10.

Feynman, Richard P. "Cornell University Lectures." 1964, NOT0.—*The Best Mind Since Einstein*, videotape, BBCIWGBI-I, Boston, 1993.

Fishburn, Peter C. Mean-Risk Analysis with Risk Associated with Below-Target Returns. *American Economic Review* 67(2) (1977): 116–126.

Fisher, Ronald A. The Statistical Utilization of Multiple Measurements. *Annals of Eugenics* 8 (1938): 376–386.

Glymour, Clark, et al. Statistical Themes and Lessons for Data Mining. *Data Mining and Knowledge Discovery*, 1 (1997): 11–28.

Goldberg, David E. Genetic Algorithms in Search, Optimization and Machine Learning. Addison-Wesley, 1989.

Goodman, Rodney M., and Padhraic Smyth. "An Information-Theoretic Model for Rule-based Expert Systems." 1988 International Symposium in Information Theory, Kobe, Japan, 1988.

Hai, Abdul, and George J. Klir. An Empirical Investigation of Reconstructability Analysis: Probabilistic System. *International Journal of Man-Machine Studies* 22 (1985): 163–192.

Han, Jiawei. Data Mining Techniques and Applications. UCLA short class, February 2–5,1998.

Harlow, W. V. Asset Allocation in a Downside-Risk Framework. *Financial Analyst Journal* 47(5) (1991): 28–40.

Harlow, W. V., and Ramesh K. S. Rao. Asset Pricing in a Generalized Mean-Lower Partial Moment Framework: Theory and Evidence. *Journal of Financial and Quantitative Analysis* 24(3) (1989): 285–311.

Hartley, Ralph V. L. Transmission of Information. *Bell Systems Technical Journal* 7 (1928): 535.

Haugen, Robert A. Building a Better Index: Cap-Weighted Benchmarks Are Inefficient Vehicles. *Pensions and Investments*, October 1, 1990.

Hogan, William W., and James M. Warren. Computation of the Efficient Boundary in the E-S Portfolio Selection Model. *Journal of Financial and Quantitative Analysis* 7(4) (1972): 1881–1896.

———. Toward the Development of an Equilibrium Capital-Market Model Based on Semi Variance." *Journal of Financial and Quantitative Analysis* 9(1) (1974): 1–11.

Hosmer, David W., and Stanley Lemeshow. *Applied Logistic Regression*. New York: Wiley, 1989.

Ibbotson, Roger G., and Paul D. Kaplan. Does Asset Allocation Policy Explain 40, 90, or 100 Percent of Performance? Yale ICF Working Paper No. 00-54. *Financial Analysts Journal* 56(1) (2000): 26–33.

Iverson, Gudmund R., and Helmut Norpoth. *Analysis of Variance*. Beverly Hills, CA: Sage Publications, 1976.

Jahnke, William W. The Asset Allocation Hoax. *Journal of Financial Planning*, February 1997: 109–113.

Johnson, Richard A., and DeanW. Wichern. *Applied Multivariate Statistical Analysis*. Englewood Cliffs, NJ: Prentice Hall, 1988.

Jones, Bush K-systems versus Classical Multivariate Systems. *International Journal of General Systems* 12 (1986): 1–6.

Jones, Bush, and Deky Gouw. The Interaction Concept of

K-systems Theory. *International Journal of General Systems*, 24 (1996): 163–169.

Joslyn, C. "Towards General Information Theoretical Representations of Database Problems." Proceedings of 1997 Conference of the IEEE Society for Systems, Man, and Cybernetics, 1997.

———. "Data Exploration through Extension and Projection." Unpublished technical report, 1998.

Kaplan, Paul D. "CFA Asset Allocation Using the Markowitz Approach." 1998.

Kaplan, Paul D., and Laurence B. Siegel. Portfolio Theory Is Alive and Well. *Journal of Investing* 3(3) (1994a): 18–23,45–46.

Klemkosky, Robert C. The Bias in Composite Performance Measures. *Journal of Financial and Quantitative Analysis* 8(3) (1973): 505–514.

Klir, George J. *Architecture of System Problem Solving*. New York: Plenum Press, 1985.

Klir, George J. On Systems Methodology and Inductive Reasoning: The Issue of Parts and Wholes. *General Systems Yearbook* 26, 29–38.

Klir, George J., and Tina Folger. *Fuzzy Sets, Uncertainty, and Information*. Englewood Cliffs, NJ: Prentice Hall, 1988.

Klir, George J., and Behzad Parviz. General Reconstruction Characteristics of Probabilistic and Possibilistic Systems. *International Journal of Man-Machine Studies* 25 (1986): 367–397.

Klir, George J., and Bo Yuan. *Fuzzy Sets and Fuzzy Logic: Theory and Applications.* Upper Saddle River, NJ: Prentice Hall, 1995.

Knoke, David, and Peter J. Burke. *Log-Linear Models.* Sage University Paper Series on Quantitative Applications in the Social Sciences, series no. 07-020. Beverly Hills and London: Sage Publications, 1980.

Kroll, Yoram, Haim Levy, and Harry M. Markowitz. "Mean-Variance Versus Direct Utility Maximization." *Journal of Finance* 39(1) (1984): 47–62.

Laughhunn, Dan J., John W. Payne, and Roy Crum. Managerial Risk Preferences for Below Target Returns. *Management Science* 26 (1980): 1238–1249.

Levitt, Arthur. *Take On The Street.* New York: Random House, 2002.

Levy, Haim, and Harry M. Markowitz. Approximating Expected Utility by a Function of Mean and Variance. *American Economic Review* 69(3) (1979): 308–317.

Lin, T. Y., and N. Cercone. *Rough Sets and Data Mining.* Norwell, MA: Kluver, 1997.

Lintner, John. The Valuation of Risk Assets and the Selection of Risky Investments in Stock Portfolios and Capital Budgets. *The Review of Economics and Statistics* 47(1) (1965): 13–37.

Lummer, Scott L. and Mark W. Riepe. "The Role of Asset Allocation in Portfolio Management." In *Global Asset Allocation: Techniques for Optimizing Portfolio Management*, edited by J. Lederman and R. Klein. New York: Wiley, 1994.

Lummer, Scott L., Mark W. Riepe, and Laurence B. Siegel. "Taming Your Optimizer: A Guide Through the Pitfalls of Mean-Variance Optimization." In *Global Asset Allocation: Techniques for Optimizing Portfolio Management*, edited by J. Lederman and R. Klein. New York: Wiley, 1994.

Mao, James C. T. Models of Capital Budgeting, E-V vs. E-S. *Journal of Financial and Quantitative Analysis* 5(5) (1970): 657–676.

Malkiel, Burton G. *A Random Walk Down Wall Street.* New York: W. W. Norton, 2003.

Markowitz, Harry M. The Early History of Portfolio Theory: 1600–1960. *Financial Analysts Journal* 55(4) (1999): 5–16.

———. *Mean-Variance Analysis in Portfolio Choice and Capital Markets.* Cambridge, MA: Basil Blackwell, 1987.

———. The Optimization of a Quadratic Function Subject to Linear Constraints. *Naval Research Logistics Quarterly* 3 (1956): 111–133.

———. Portfolio Selection. *Journal of Finance* 7(1) (1952): 77–91.

———. *Portfolio Selection,* 1st ed. New York: John Wiley, 1959.

———. *Portfolio Selection,* 2nd ed. Cambridge, MA: Basil Blackwell, 1991.

Martin, J. Kent. An Exact Probability Metric for Decision Tree Splitting and Stopping. *Machine Learning* 28 (1997): 257–291.

McCulloch, Warren S. and Walter Pitts. A Logical Calculus of the Ideas Immanent in Neuron Activity. *Bulletin of Mathematical Biophysics,* 5 (1943): 115–133.

Miller, Irwin, John E. Freund, and Richard A. Johnson. *Probability and Statistics for Engineers,* 4th ed. Englewood Cliffs, NJ: Prentice Hall, 1990.

Mitchell, Melanie. *An Introduction to Genetic Algorithms.* Boston: MIT Press, 1996.

Mossin, Jan. Equilibrium in a Capital Asset Market. *Econometrica* 34 (1966): 768–783.

Motwani, Rajeev, Sergey Brin, and Craig Silverstein. "Beyond Market Baskets: Generalizing Association Rules to Correlation." 1997 ACM SIGMOD Conference on Management of Data, 1997, 265-276.

Nantell, Timothy J., and Barbara Price. An Analytical Comparison of Variance and Semi Variance Capital Market Theories. *Journal of Financial and Quantitative Analysis* 14(2) (1979): 221–242.

Nawrocki, David. The Characteristics of Portfolios Selected by n-Degree Lower Partial Moment. *International Review of Financial Analysis* 1(3) (1992): 195–210.

———. A Comparison of Risk Measures When Used in a Simple Portfolio Selection Heuristic. *Journal of Business Finance and Accounting* 10(2) (1983): 183–194.

———. Optimal Algorithms and Lower Partial Moment: Ex Post Results. *Applied Economics* 23(3) (1991): 465–470.

———. Tailoring Asset Allocation to the Individual Investor. *International Review of Economics and Business* 38(10-11) (1990): 977–990.

Nawrocki, David, and Katharine Staples. A Customized LPM Risk Measure for Portfolio Analysis. *Applied Economics* 21(2) (1989): 205–218.

Nilsson, Nils J. *Learning Machines: Foundations of Trainable Pattern-Classifying Systems*. New York: McGraw-Hill, 1965.

Pandya, Abhijit S., and Robert B. Macy. *Pattern Recognition with Neural Networks in C++*. Boca Raton, FL: CRC-Press, 1996.

Philippatos, George C. "Computer Programs for Implementing Portfolio Theory." Unpublished Software, Pennsylvania State University, 1971.

Piatetsky-Shapiro, Gregory, and William J. Frawley, eds. *Knowledge Discovery in Databases*. Menlo Park, CA: AAAI Press/MIT Press, 1991.

Pittarelli, Michael. An Algebra for Probabilistic Databases. *IEEE Transactions on Knowledge and Data Engineering* 6 (1994): 293–303.

———. A Note on Probability Estimation Using Reconstructability Analysis. *International Journal of General Systems* 18 (1990): 11–21.

Popper, Karl R. *The Logic of Scientific Discovery*. New York: Routledge, 1959.

Porter, R. Burr. Semi Variance and Stochastic Dominance: A Comparison. *American Economic Review* 64(1)(1974): 200–204.

Porter, R. Burr, James R. Wart, and Donald L. Ferguson. Efficient Algorithms for Conducting Stochastic Dominance Tests on Large Numbers of Portfolios. *Journal of Financial and Quantitative Analysis* 8(1) (1973): 71–81.

Porter, R. Burr, and Roger P. Bey. An Evaluation of the Empirical Significance of Optimal Seeking Algorithms in Portfolio Selection. *Journal of Finance* 29(5) (1974), 1479–1490.

Quinlan, J. Ross. Induction of Decision Trees. *Machine Learning* 1, 81–106.

Quirk, James P., and Rubin Saposnik. Admissibility and Measurable Utility Functions. *Review of Economic Studies* 29 (1962).

Ramsey, Dave. *Financial Peace Planner*. New York: Penguin, 1998.

———. *How to Have More Than Enough*. New York: Penguin, 1999.

———. *The Total Money Makeover*. Nashville: Thomas Nelson Publishing, 2003.

Rom, Brian M., and Kathleen W. Ferguson. Portfolio Theory Is Alive and Well: A Response. *Journal of Investing* 3(3) (1994b): 24–44.

———. Post-Modern Portfolio Theory Comes of Age. *Journal of Investing* 3(3) (1994a): 11–17.

———. Using Post-Modern Portfolio Theory to Improve Investment Performance Measurement. *Journal of Performance Measurement* 2(2)(1997/1998): 5–13.

Ross, Stephen A. The Capital Asset Pricing Model (CAPM), Short-Sale Restrictions and Related Issues. *Journal of Finance* 32 (1977): 177–183.

Roy, A. D. Safety First and the Holding of Assets. *Econometrica* 20(3) (1952): 431–449.

Shannon, Claude E. A Mathematical Theory of Communication. *The Bell Systems Technical Journal* 27 (1948): 379–423.

Sharpe, William F. Capital Asset Prices: A Theory of Market Equilibrium under Conditions of Risk. *Journal of Finance* 19(3)(1964): 425–442.

———. A Linear Programming Algorithm for Mutual Fund Portfolio Selection. *Management Science* 13(7) (1967): 499–510.

———. Mutual Fund Performance. *Journal of Business* 39(1)(1966): 119–138.

Sharpe, William F., and Gordon J. Alexander. *Investments*, 4th ed. Englewood Cliffs, NJ: Prentice Hall, 1990.

Shen, Wei- Min, et al. "An Overview of Database Mining Techniques." http://www.isi. edu/ ~shen/Tsur.ps.

Silver, Lloyd. Risk Assessment for Security Analysis. *Technical Analysis of Stocks and Commodities*. January 1993: 74–79.

Simon, Herbert A. A Behavioral Model of Rational Choice. *Quarterly Journal of Economics* 69(1) (1955): 99–118.

Smyth, P., and Goodman, R. M. An Information Theoretic Approach to Rule Induction from Databases. *IEEE Transactions on Knowledge and Data Engineering* 4 (1992): 301–316.

Sortino, Frank A., and Hal J. Forsey. On the Use and Misuse of Downside Risk. *Journal of Portfolio Management* 22(2)(1996): 35–42.

Sortino, Frank A., and Lee N. Price. Performance Measurement in a Downside Risk Framework. *Journal of Investing* 3(3) (1994): 59–64.

Sortino, Frank A., and Robert Van Der Meer. Downside Risk. *Journal of Portfolio Management* 17(4)(1991): 27–32.

Srikant, Ramakrishnan, and Rakesh Agrawal. "Mining Generalized Association Rules." Proceedings of the 21st VLDB Conference, Zurich, Switzerland, 1995.

Surz, Ronald J., Dale H. Stevens, and Mark E. Wimer. The Importance of Investment Policy. *Journal of Investing* 8(4)(1999).

Swaim, Ralph O. Utility Theory-Insights Into Risk Taking. *Harvard Business Review* 44(6) (1966): 123–138.

Tobin, James. Liquidity Preference as Behavior Towards Risk. *The Review of Economic Studies* 25(2) (1958): 65–86.

The Vanguard Group Inc. "Sources of Portfolio Performance: The Enduring Importance of Asset Allocation." July 2003.

Veelentwurf, L. P. J. *Analysis and Applications of Artificial Neural Networks*. Hertfordshire, UK: Prentice Hall, 1995.

Von Neumann, John, and Oskar Morgenstern. *Theory of Games and Economic Behavior*. Princeton, NJ: Princeton University Press, 1944.

Wasserman, Philip D. *Advanced Methods in Neural Computing*. New York: Van Nostrand Reinhold, 1993.

Weiss, Gary. *Wall Street Versus America*. New York: Penguin Publishing Group, 2006.

Wellstock, Peter S. *Against the Gods: The Remarkable Story of Risk*. New York: Wiley, 1996.

———. *Capital Ideas: The Improbable Origins of Modern Wall Street*. New York: The Free Press, 1993.

Zwick, Martin, Hui Shu, and Roy Koch. Information-Theoretic Mask Analysis of Rainfall Time Series Data. *Advances in System Science and Application* 1 (1995): 154–159.

# ROBERT KNEISLEY

## About the Author

Bob began his financial services career in 1972. He is a native Toledoan and a graduate of the University of Toledo. He is a charter member of Authors on the Net and author of *The Indicator!* and *Wall Street Casino*. He was a charter member of the Toledo Chapter of the International Association of Financial Planners and is a Pension Consultant accredited by the National Institute of Pension Administrators. He has participated in numerous panel discussions and has generated many newspaper and magazine articles, audio tapes, and CDs concerning financial matters. He has been published in *Financial Planning* magazine, the *Advisor Network* and various trade publications. Mr. Kneisley is a member in good standing of the National Institute of Pension Administrators, the Profit Sharing Council of America, Ohio

# THE WALL STREET CASINO

State University/Toledo Sea Grant Advisory Committee, and founder of the Winning Investment Network. Bob is also known as the "Investor's Ally" with a web site at www.investorsally.net.

Early on, Bob recognized the need for education in support of efficient investing and independent, <u>fee-only</u> consulting. He established the Indicator Advisory Corporation in 1986 to meet the demand for a research oriented, <u>very independent</u> advisory service. His firm serves as a consultant <u>to the client</u>—not some distant corporation. The firm's aim is to offer the most academically advanced, competitive, institutional quality products and services to his corporate, pension, and individual investors. In addition, the firm serves the needs of <u>fee-only</u> trade professionals. Mr. Kneisley's select clientele enjoy the reality of his firm's philosophy.

# Index

## A

active investing 4, 5, 7, 165
analysts ix, x, xxiv, 6, 13, 14, 27, 57, 77, 114, 125, 127
asset allocation 9, 10, 73, 76, 87, 107, 140
Asset Allocation 165
asset class 10, 79, 81, 106, 107, 125, 144
Asset Class 145

## B

banking xxii, 73, 122
bear market xi, 3
Bogle, John xv
bonds xi, xii, xx, 3, 10, 21, 57, 122, 165, 166, 167, 170, 173, 174, 175, 176, 177, 179, 180, 181, 182
break point 78
break points 78
brokerage house vii, ix, x, xi, xiii, xv, xx, xxii, xxiii, xxiv, 1, 2, 5, 6, 21, 23, 24, 25, 27, 74, 75, 78, 105, 137, 139, 176, 179
broker/dealer xiii, xxiii, 4, 5, 75, 139

## C

call options 21, 26
Capital Asset Pricing Model 77, 107, 196
capital gains tax 107
clearing costs 7, 21, 74
commission ix, xxiii, 1, 6, 73, 78, 169, 170, 171, 175, 177, 179
compound interest 2, 57, 58

## D

determination & probability 59, 194
discarding xxv
distribution xxiv, xxv, 167, 170, 181
diversification 9, 10, 73, 107, 170
dividends xii, 166, 170, 173, 177, 181

## E

Efficient Market Hypothesis 77
expense ratio 7, 9, 21, 74, 140

## F

fee-only xiii, xix, 78, 107, 202
free markets 57, 62, 91, 92, 94, 124

## G

growth stocks 173

## H

herding 106
hidden fees 78

## I

independent advice xv, 28, 77
index funds 71
inflation xxi, 7, 121, 122
infrastructure 61, 110, 121
interest x, xi, xii, xiii, 2, 57, 58, 62, 73, 136, 166, 168, 170, 172, 173, 174, 177, 181, 182
investment advisor xxiv, 24, 78, 107

investment efficiency 45
investor behavior 108, 198

**L**

labor organizations 91, 110, 123
law of large numbers 59

**M**

market impact 94
marketing fees 75, 78, 138, 169
market timing xix, 77
Markowitz, Harry 107
Modern Portfolio Theory xix, 107, 125, 135, 196
Morningstar 60, 74
mortgage xxii, 73, 173
municipal bonds xx, 181
mutual funds xxii, xxiii, 7, 10, 21, 59, 74, 75, 78, 107, 127, 137, 140, 172, 175, 180

**N**

Nobel laureates 77
Nobel Prize 136

**P**

passive investing 7, 8, 24, 29, 45, 71, 107, 124, 176
past performance xix
portfolio turnover 2
prospectus 139, 140, 174, 177

**R**

real estate xx, xxi, 10, 26, 172, 178
rebalancing 73
retail brokerage industry 6, 22
rotation xxiv

**S**

securities viii, xv, xxi, 1, 5, 8, 10, 72, 107, 165, 167, 168, 169, 170, 171, 173, 174, 175, 176, 177, 178, 179, 180, 181, 182
Securities & Exchange Commission 171, 179
Sharpe, William 107, 136, 196, 197
shelf space 75
S&P 500 127, 180
standard of living 5, 6
Statement of Additional Information 139
stock picking xix, 77
stocks ix, xi, xii, xxiii, 3, 10, 21, 27, 57, 59, 74, 89, 127, 140, 166, 169, 170, 171, 173, 174, 175, 176, 177, 179, 197

**T**

taxation 123, 178
tax-deductible 22, 174
total return 126
Trim Tabs xxv

**U**

University of Chicago 77, 107

**V**

volatility 10, 57, 107, 135, 136, 166, 182

**W**

Weiss, Gary 198

# Subject Index

## Symbols

79th Street Marina  131
401(k)  70, 82, 84, 86, 87, 172

## A

AARP  130
Adjustable rate mortgages  74
Africans  61, 62
Agricultural Age  54
AIDS  65
AllCan.org  161, 162
AllCan Workshop Series  164
American Stock Exchange  132
Apartheid system  65
Aquarius  43, 44, 60, 61, 89, 90, 108, 119, 131, 147, 148, 149
Archimedes  57
Asia  90
Asian Financial Crisis  122
Asset class index funds  71, 106
Atlantic Ocean  62, 131
Australia  62
Auto Africa Expo Show  47
Averaging down  100

## B

Bay of Edo  91
Bering Sea  125
Berlin Wall  113
Bertha's Restaurant  62
Bid/ask price  85
Big Spender  128
Bogle, John C.  xv, 68
Boston College  85
Break points  78
Brignoles  47
Brinson, Hood and Beebower  76
British Empire  61
British Prime Minister Margaret Thatcher  93
British Rule  63
Brokerage firms  74
Brokerage house  75
Bubble  106

## C

Cape of Good Hope  62
Cape Sable  148
Cape Town  44, 60, 61, 63, 80
Capital Asset Pricing Model  77, 107
Caribbean Sea  131
China  42, 90, 91, 92, 93, 94, 96
Chinese Civil War  94
Christ  54
Clearing costs  85
Clearing fee  74
Commodities Futures Trading Commission (CFTC)  153
Commodore Matthew Perry  91
Communist North Korea  92
Communist Party  112
Communist Party of China  94
Compound interest  57
Computer Age  55
Congress of New York  133

## D

Dartmouth  136
Department of Labor  84
Determination and probability  59
Disposition effect  100

Dow Jones Industrial Average 144
Duke of York 71

# E

East River 131
Economic delta 117
Edelen, Roger 85
Efficient Frontier Newsletter 7
Efficient Market Hypothesis 77
Egyptians 82
Einstein, Albert 57
Evans, Richard 85
e.Volution 47
Expense ratio 74, 85, 140

# F

Fama, Eugene F. 144
Far East 93
FDIC "Watch List" 162
Federal Reserve 74
Fee-only investment advisors 107
Felix Wankel 47
Figby & Prentice 137
Fixed income 114
Flexible commissions 73
France 47
Fraunce's Tavern 132, 133, 147
Fraunce, Sam 133
Freedom of Information Act 160

# G

Goldman, Marshall 122
Gorbachev, Mikhail 121
Great Wall of China 91

# H

Halifax 149
Herd mentality 106
Hidden fees 78

Hindsight bias 101
Hong Kong 80, 90, 92, 93, 94, 103, 112
Hood 76
Hormel Foods 126
House money 100
Hyundai Hotel 111

# I

Ibbotson Associates 99
Indemac Bank 162
Indonesia 92
Information Age 55
Iinsider privatization 122
Internet 161
Intrinsic value 13, 144
Investor Behavioral Finance 97

# J

Jacobs, Malcolm 63
Japan 91
J. Faraday 46
Jumbo floating restaurant 96

# K

Kadlec, Gregory 85
Kiwanis 95
Korea 92

# L

Labor unions 91
Lake Erie 148
Law of large numbers 59
Legal persons 93
LLC 137
Loss aversion 98

# M

M-2 money supply 160
Mancini, Henry 96

Manhattan Island  71
MarketBrowser.com  160
Market impact  79
Marketing fees  75
Market returns  79
Market timing  79
Market Timing  76
Market volatility  79
Mark Twain  55
Markowitz, Harry  32, 107
May Day  73
Media response syndrome  106
Mental accounting  100
Metals Age  54
Model T Ford  47
Modern Portfolio Theory  32, 107, 135
Moon River  96
Morningstar  60, 69, 74, 87
Motorola  125
Mozambique  65

## N

NAFTA  91
Napoleon Hill  46
Narrow framing  100
NASDAQ  73
Nazi invasion  121
Negative coefficients  107
Negotiated commissions  73
New Amsterdam  71
New Netherlands  71
New York  72
New York Bay  131
New York Chamber of Commerce  133
New York City  131
New York Stock Board  72
New York Stock Exchange  72
Nicholas Otto  47
Nile Delta  82

Nobel Prize  136
North America  163
Nova Scotia  149

## O

Obie, Stephen J.  160
Old Tokyo  91

## P

Pacific  131
Panama Canal  131
Paris  127
Passive investing  71
Pavlov's  6
People's Republic of China  93
Perestroika  121
Peter Minuit  71
Pettiford, Valarie  128
Pieces of eight  72
POGO  117
Pokrovsky Park  110
Portugal  65
Professor Maboto  62
Profit Sharing Council  86
Profit Sharing Council of America  84, 201
Prospectus  139
Put options  89

## Q

Quantity discounts  78
Quarterdeck Club  94
Quick cash sites  114

## R

Rasmussen, Reggie  134
Reflections on the Motive Power of Fire  47
Renaissance Age  54
Renaissance Harbour Hotel  96

Revolutionary War  133
Rex Sinquefield  81
Risk premium  136
Risk/return  145
Rolls Royc  132
Rotary  95
Russia  108, 112
Russian Central Banking System  122
Russian Financial Crisis  122

## S

Sadi Carnot  47
Sakoko  91
Sales commission  85
Savery, Thomas  46
Scale Effects of Mutual Fund Performance  85
Scotland  109
Scots  72
SEC  85
Second World War  121
Securities and Exchange Commission  135
Shanghai Stock Exchange  93
Sharpe, Dr. William  136
Sharpe's measure  136
Sharpe, William F.  107
Shrill, Dr. William  124, 132
Simon's Town  62
Singapore  92
Socialism  96
Sons of Liberty  133
South Africa  44, 47, 60, 62, 63, 82, 112
South Atlantic  108
South Korea  92
Sovietologist  122
Soviet Union  112
S&P 500  127
Spam  126

Spanish currency  72
Stalin Era  120
Stalin, Joseph  120
Standard deviation  99
Stanford University  107
Statement of Additional Information  139
State Planning Committee  120
Statue of Liberty  127
Stirling engine  46
St. Lawrence Seaway  148
Stockjobbers  71, 73
Stock Picking  76
Stone Age  54
Storchak, Professor Ivan  111
Strait of La Perouse  125

## T

Taiwan  94
Target funds  87
Tati Valley  62
Tax deductible  78
Thatcher, Margaret  93
The Good, the Bad and the Ugly  140
The Big Apple  127
The Good  140
The Wealth of Nations  72
Think and Grow Rich!  46
Toledo, Ohio  148
Track Record  76
Transportation Age  55
Transvaal  62

## U

United Kingdom  93
United State  66
University of Chicago  77
University of Virginia  85
Stanford University  107
U.S. Treasury Department  73

## V

Vaal Valley  62
Vanguard Mutual Fund  68
Victoria Harbour  94, 95, 97
Virginia Tech  85
Vladivostok  108, 110, 131
Volatility  10, 24, 34, 35, 56, 57, 79, 99, 107, 117, 135, 136, 166, 182
Voucher fund  121

## W

Wall Street  72, 77
Wall Street Casino  131, 134
Wall Street Versus America  135
Wanchai  94
War Bond  160
War of 1812  72
Warren Buffet  37, 132
Washington, George  133
Washington Room  133
water people  96
Weiss, Gary  135
Wellstock  137
Wellstock, Mr. Graven  137
Widow's Fund  72
William J. Bernstein  7
William Sturgeon  46
Will Rogers  140
Willy Wonka and the Chocolate Factory  92
Wrap fee account  139
Wray, David L.  86

## X

Xiamggang  90

## Y

Yellow Sea  108
Yeltsin, Boris  113, 121

## Z

Zero Pollution Motors  47

# THE WALL STREET CASINO

# Source Credits

## Vanguard

"Vanguard" is a trademark of The Vanguard Group, Inc. © 2007 The Vanguard Group, Inc. All rights reserved. Reprinted with permission. Subject to the terms and conditions of this Permissions Agreement dated 4-1-08, The Vanguard Group, Inc. ("Vanguard") grants Publisher the nonexclusive, nontransferable, limited right to publish the Work in the United States as part of the English edition of the above-described publication. Publisher may not use the Work in any subsequent edition or release of the Publication, or in any other media, whether such media exists today or is developed in the future, without obtaining Vanguard's prior written permission. Vanguard will not charge a fee for granting Publisher this limited right to publish the Work in the Publication.

## Fotosearch

The current document is made to confirm that you are allowed to use all three images in a book and in DVDs. However, you have read the license agreements to know any restrictions or conditions that may apply. These license agreements are available on www.fotosearch.com under the Licensing section. With all advantages thereto pertaining.

## Dalbar, Inc.

This book includes data generated by DALBAR, Inc. and presented in their DALBAR 2008 Quantitative Analysis of Investor Behavior Study."

Used by permission of Standard & Poor's. SPIVA® is a registered trademark of McGraw-Hill Companies, Inc. All Rights Reserved.

**Passive Investing Study**
**C.D. $17.95 + 2.50 Shipping & Handling**
**Call for bulk book pricing**
**1-800-547-7888**

ORDER TOLL FREE

Technical Financial Publishing
P.O. Box 5194
Toledo, OH 43611
1-800-547-7888

Please call for bulk pricing of CDs and books. A custom book design is available to <u>fee-only</u>, licensed investment advisory firms, corporations, and schools for educational purposes.

---

Please send me \_\_\_\_\_ copies of the paperback edition of *The Wall Street Casino* at $23.00 each, which includes shipping and handling. Enclosed is my check for $_____

**Signature** _____

**Name** _____

**Address** _____

**City** _____ **State** _____ **Zip** _____

Phone _____

e-Mail _____

Please visit us on the web at http://www.investorsally.net.

Printed in the United States
130260LV00002BA/3/P